ACTION GUIDE SERIES

TINNA C. NIE

# Action Guide
# Inclusion Nudges for Talent Selection

**in all organisations and communities**

**30 Inclusive Actions**
De-biasing processes to recruit, promote, and enhance
the diversity of talents of all people
by applying Inclusion Nudges

**Authors of The Inclusion Nudges Guidebook (2020)**
**Authors of the Inclusion Nudges Action Guide Series**
**Founders of the Inclusion Nudges Global Initiative & Community**
www.inclusion-nudges.org
contact@inclusion-nudges.org

**Tinna C. Nielsen**
Founder, Move the Elephant for Inclusiveness
www.movetheelephant.org

**Lisa Kepinski**
Founder, Inclusion Institute
www.inclusion-institute.com

**Inclusion Nudges for Talent Selection Action Guide**
August 2020
© Tinna C. Nielsen & Lisa Kepinski
ISBN: 9798679411005
KDP

Book cover art & icon design by Ruth Crone Foster
www.ruthcronefoster.dk
Book design by Christina Hucke
www.christinahucke.de

Great talent selection is critical
for success in teams, projects, change,
organisations, and communities.

Accessing and leveraging
the full diversity of talents is a must.

This Action Guide
makes it easy for you to do this.

# Table of Contents

| | |
|---|---|
| **What People Say About Inclusion Nudges** | 7 |
| Section 1: **Great Talent Selection Is Inclusive** | 17 |
| Section 2: **Insights About the Human Mind** | 25 |
| Section 3: **How to Change Absurd Realities to Great Talent Selection** | 47 |
| Section 4: **The Power of the Inclusion Nudges Change Approach** | 53 |
| Section 5: **Inclusive Actions for Talent Selection** | 65 |
| Section 6: **How You Take This Forward** | 209 |
| **Reference Section** | 225 |
| About the Authors | 227 |
| Endnotes | 230 |

..............................................................................

*The majority of the actions in this Action Guide are from* The Inclusion Nudges Guidebook *(2020) by Lisa Kepinski & Tinna C. Nielsen.*

*To learn more about the Inclusion Nudges global initiative and community, go to the website. There you will find more resources to support you, including about* The Inclusion Nudges Guidebook *and the other books in the Action Guide Series.*

*Learn more at the Inclusion Nudges resource platform*
www.inclusion-nudges.org

# The Inclusion Nudges Global Initiative & Change Approach

Let's make inclusion the norm – everywhere, for everyone

### Why
There is a need to leverage the diverse human potential of everyone to co-create inclusive organisations, communities, and society

### What
Inclusion Nudges are behavioural designs to debias and enhance inclusive collaboration, leadership, development, and decisions

### How
Empowering you to apply Inclusion Nudges to engage all people in making systems, cultures, and behaviours inclusive as the norm

# What people say about INCLUSION NUDGES

"*The Inclusion Nudges Guidebook* shows how practitioners can use behavioral insights to create more inclusive, more diverse, and better organizations. I recommend it to all who care and want to make a difference."

**Iris Bohnet**
Albert Pratt Professor of Business & Government and
Co-director, Women & Public Policy Program
Kennedy School of Government, Harvard University,
Author of *What Works: Gender Equality by Design*, U.S.


"Many people now understand bias but are still searching for truly effective ways to reduce it. This refreshing and timely book is filled with behavioral science-based practical examples, referred to as 'Inclusion Nudges', that are designed for easy use by people in their organizations and communities to de-bias, reduce harassment and create greater inclusion. It's time to move from discussing to acting, and that's what *The Inclusion Nudges Guidebook* will help you to do."

**Amy Cuddy**
Social psychologist, author, speaker, & Harvard University lecturer,
Author of *Presence*, U.S.


"*The Inclusion Nudges Guidebook* is an eye-opener for the importance and concrete benefits of de-biasing and inclusion."

**Katja Pehrman**
Senior Adviser for UN Women
The United Nations


"Inclusion Nudges are not just the innovation we need today; they're a blueprint for a future in which we are designing organizations and communities to be more inclusive from the get-go rather than as an overlay or afterthought."

**Minjon Tholen**
Chief Inclusion & Strategic Innovation Officer
Amnesty International, U.S.


"The more I learn about the social change sector the more I see how valuable are Tinna Nielsen & Lisa Kepinski's insights and Inclusion Nudges!"

**Francesca Folda**
Journalist, social entrepreneur, & Director of Global Communications
Amani Institute, Italy

"What if we're going about this inclusion thing all wrong? This the gently persuasive idea behind Inclusion Nudges…co-founded by Lisa Kepinski and Tinna Nielsen, two experts who were looking for a better way. They share what they learn freely and invite others to do the same via their open-source platform … I plan to nudge my way to a more open mind. We all should."[1]

**Ellen McGirt**
Senior Editor, Fortune Magazine & Co-chair, The CEO Initiative, U.S.


"Tinna Nielsen and Lisa Kepinski have grabbed the tiger the tail with their excellent work on Inclusion Nudges. By doing exhaustive research on not only what can work, but also what is actually working, they have put together a powerful toolkit that not only helps people discover behaviors that can encourage a more inclusive environment, but also shapes our thinking in ways that help us learn to find new solutions ourselves. This is an important book for anyone who wants to create real, sustainable change in their organization."

**Howard Ross**
Founder Cook Ross, consultant, & speaker,
Author of *Our Search for Belonging* and *Everyday Bias,* Founder Udarta Consulting, U.S.


"*The Inclusion Nudges Guidebook* is a wonderful resource full of practical advice. Above all its greatest value is in demonstrating that bias can be addressed."

**Binna Kandola**
Business psychologist, professor, consultant, & speaker
Author of *Racism at Work* and *Invention of Difference*
Pearn Kandola, U.K.


"One of my favourite aspects of *The Inclusion Nudges Guidebook* is the 100+ concrete examples it presents that have been proven to lead people willingly toward more inclusive behaviour. These really do work. As such, the Guidebook is an evidence-based powerful tool to inspire the use of these and other nudges to make sustainable change in organisations and communities."

**Ursula Wynhoven**
Leader advancing social sustainability & gender equality initiatives
The United Nations

"Inclusion Nudges changed my view on how to approach inclusion & gender equity."
**Claire Bonenfant**
Country Director, SThree, France


"What Tinna, Lisa, and their community have created is a true public good: a collection of practical, implementable case studies grounded in experiences in the real world which others can learn from. I commend their work and recommend *The Inclusion Nudges Guidebook* to anyone passionate about inclusivity."
**Kate Glazebrook**
CEO & Co-founder, Applied, U.K.
& previously U.K. Behavioural Insights Team


"Governments around the world are more and more considering and using behavioural insights to improve the lives of citizens. The Inclusion Nudge Guidebook is a good resource for public servants interested in learning more about how to have a more inclusive society."
**Lisa Witter**
Executive Chairperson and Co-founder
Apolitical, Germany


"Are you ready to debunk and interrupt your biases? Use the well-researched practical Inclusion Nudges in this great guidebook!"
**Mumbi Mbocha**
Diversity & Inclusion Officer, The United Nation's World Food Programme


"Inclusion Nudges help enable leaders to move from general awareness to catalyst agents for inclusion & diversity. The ideas are simple and immediately actionable, with several members of my team immediately incorporating changes in their day to day leadership."
**Kaye DeLange**
Vice President for Salt Business Operations and Supply Chain Leader
Cargill, U.S.


"Inclusion Nudges have made a big difference for me in my work."
**Magda Kanjejo**
Social Entrepreneur, Kenya

"After so much communication by experts and "sponsors" to state the importance of diversity and after so many hours of D&I training to increase the awareness, I always wondered how long-lasting change in behaviour can be truly achieved. Lisa Kepinski and Tinna Nielsen's full version of *The Inclusion Nudges Guidebook* not only gives some idea, but it provides a very well structured and supported reference library of 100 potential solutions. And do you still feel stuck to make the change? Detailed stuck patterns are included!"
**Endre Szabo**
Senior Vice President, Managing Director, Developing Europe & Africa Region
Brown-Forman, The Netherlands


"*The Inclusion Nudges Guidebook* is a brilliant book full of tons of little things that can be done in all situations to nudge people's thinking and actions to be inclusive. It's a great book for anyone working on inclusion and diversity."
**Sarah Bakewell**
Diversity & Inclusion Manager, AWE, U.K.


"The work by Tinna Nielsen and Lisa Kepinski on Inclusion Nudges exemplifies how behavioural science offers powerful tools to change the world for the better. After all, what on earth would you look at when you want to change behaviour, if not precisely how behaviour works? And the work of Inclusion Nudges is at the forefront of this."
**Federico Raimondi**
Head & Founder of $R^2$ - Office of Behavioural Policy, City of Rome, Italy


"Inclusion is one of the most important things to be mindful of in the tech industry. Stereotypes may influence with whom and how we may work. It is a waste of potential, resources, and money, not to include everyone. It is our responsibility as leaders, founders, and C-levels to include everyone in our organisations. It's not only about team building; it is also about growing the company. There is no growth without the team. There is no team without inclusion. The Inclusion Nudges approach offers many ways to make this happen in our organisations. I have used some of these approaches to great impact within my own company, and I encourage others to try this as well."
**Bartek Jazwinski**
Co-founder, Perfect Dashboard, Poland

"*The Inclusion Nudges Guidebook* is invaluable to me. I highly recommend it for people leaders. It is laid out in such a way that anyone can pick it up and easily find a nudge that will help to start the conversation around inclusion and diversity. A must have in any leadership toolbox."
**Kevin Bradley**
Senior Advisor, Global Inclusion & Diversity, Zebra Technologies, U.S.


"To limit bias damage, I asked around for practical tools, but felt many are stuck in the 'men are evil' discussion. However, I was so pleased to finally get a hold of *The Inclusion Nudges Guidebook*. Thanks a million!"
**Emma Hammarlund**
Geo-biologist, lecturer, & researcher at Translational Cancer Research,
Lund University, Sweden
& The Nordic Center for Earth Evolution, Southern Denmark


"Many believe that creating a more inclusive workplace requires costly D&I programs and massive culture change efforts over months or years. *The Inclusion Nudges Guidebook* offers powerful and proven actions that have an extraordinary impact and can be done today for very little investment. It has become one of the most useful references in my library. I have incorporated a number of Inclusion Nudges into my presentations and strategies on diversity and inclusion within the company. It has been a great practical way of getting to action, rather than just talk. It's a fantastic book that really brings behavioural economics into the world of Inclusion & Diversity. I highly recommend it for anyone in a D&I role."
**Guy Martin**
Global HR Program Director, ASSA ABLOY Global Solutions, Denmark


"*The Inclusion Nudges Guidebook* is in the top 5 of the list that I give to people who ask for good books to read."
**Marc Bernardin**
Associate Director, Accordia, France


"I find this to be a great resource to nudge individuals towards inclusion. By using the examples from *The Inclusion Nudges Guidebook*, the road to true inclusion becomes less bumpy."
**Rashmi Vikram**
Former global D&I leader for Microsoft & Community Business, India

"*The Inclusion Nudges Guidebook* is my go-to resource to create behavioral nudges to increase diversity, mitigate bias, and create a culture of belonging. The nudges are practical, easy to apply or adapt, and based on the science of how our brains works. Whether diversity and inclusion is your full-time job or you are a business leader that cares deeply about this topic, this book gives you the most bang for your buck!"
**Scott Ballina**
Senior Director, Diversity & Inclusion, Citrix, U.S.

"We have benefitted happily from using Inclusion Nudges. It has ensured a systematic run-through of many perspectives which we would not necessarily have addressed, had it not been for this [design and change methodology] model. The model has facilitated effective and rich proposals and solutions with broad applicability in a number of instances. The model proves its value by enabling us to be precise and focused in our strategic initiative."
**Eva Sophia Myers**
Leader for Gender Equality Team,
Coordinator for SPEAR (EU), University of Southern Denmark

"Inclusion Nudges took our perspective of implementing more inclusive practices from a chore to an eye-opening celebration of others and their potential to help us achieve our joint goals."
**Samantha McKinnon Brown**
Meeting Professionals International Northern California Chapter (MPINCC)
Chair of Membership Retention, U.S.

"Inclusion Nudges has helped me take the blame out my challenge to inspire organizations to become more inclusive. Learning the science behind bias and learned behaviour has made me a more effective advocate in the field of Diversity, Equity, & Inclusion because I can put more action and objectives to implementation. A nudge is always better than pushing aggressively. Inclusion Nudges is a brilliant concept that inspires advocates like me to be patient yet strategic with encouraging change … [and] speak in a more loving and nudging manner."
**Zoe Moore**
Inclusion & Diversity Consultant, U.S.

"Implicit biases influence our judgement and decision-making. They affect our choices about who to work, play, and partner with, education and careers. They can influence who we hire, promote, and reward, and where we allocate precious resources. This is important to IBM, as to any business dealing with people. Once we're aware of our biases, Inclusion Nudges are a way of achieving a more adequate behaviour. We want to develop these skills in IBM Denmark, and therefore we have trained a team of champions who can work with Inclusion Nudges throughout the organisation."

**Ulla Dalsgaard**
Nordic Learning Partner, IBM, Denmark


"Inclusion Nudges are instrumental to providing sustainability for a culture of inclusion. For years, we have focused on raising awareness of bias and what a culture of inclusion 'looks like' but Inclusion Nudges provide the pathway for implementing the behaviors that sustain the culture we are seeking."

**Eric Dziedzic**
Vice President, Diversity & Inclusion, Charter Communications
President & Founder, CRx Solutions, U.S.


"We applied an Inclusion Nudge and it was an eye-opener for them, as well as for me, to have them experience in a simple, yet very strong, manner what happens when they work. The exercise and the experience made a strong impact that left them motivated to nudge themselves to change own unconscious pattern."

**Kirsten Barslund**
Organisational Development & Diversity Specialist in the film industry, Denmark


"Leaders can embody social courage through their workplace actions. A first step is to implement Inclusion Nudges. Sounds too simple perhaps but the results are profound."

**Jo Ann Morris**
Founder of Integral Coaching,
Author of *Ignite: Inspiring Courageous Leaders*, and
Co-Founder of White Men as Full Diversity Partners, U.S.

SECTION 1

# Great Talent Selection Is Inclusive

> Why it matters that you are INCLUSIVE in your talent selection

This *Action Guide for Talent Selection* gives you 30 Inclusion Nudges, which are designs based on insights from behavioural sciences and expertise about bias, diversity, equity, and inclusion. This is not a guide that describes a recruitment process step-by-step with all the practices, tools, and processes needed to be successful. This guide gives you 30 proven-to-work inclusive behavioural designs on how to mitigate bias and make talent selection inclusive through the entire process, step-by-step. Consider it a supplement and a game changer.

This Action Guide is for you who are involved in selecting people for jobs, promotions, community initiatives, change efforts and composing great diverse teams or in any other way involved in talent (people) selection processes in your organisation, initiative, change effort, or community. Getting this right pays off.

The value proposition is clear cut and proven. Not only is it important to select the right person for the task, role, team, it is just as critical if not more important to have a diverse make-up in the team to reach the best solutions. 'The best solution' is no longer only for what's best for your own community, organisation, business, and bottom line, but it's also as much for the social and societal impact that it has. Collectively, we have a need for the outcomes to be as diverse and inclusive as possible due to the scale and pace of changes with which we are faced.

## The world is changing and new solutions are needed

Rarely have organisations around the world agreed so closely on the growing need for more inclusive collaboration and inclusive growth as a means to solving the new challenges we are facing in the labour market, in our workplaces, in our institutions, in our governments, and in our communities. Our current time in history is called The Fourth Industrial Revolution and is characterised by technology, artificial intelligence, robotics, and machine learning. This, together with the global pandemic, people's demands for greater equity and inclusion, and concerns for the environmental crisis, all point to the need for new solutions. The response to these massive social, environmental, educational, health, economic, employment, and political challenges is being called The Great Reset[2]. The call to action from the United Nations, the European Union, the World Economic Forum, the World Bank, the OECD, the IMF, and many others is one that can unite us all.

> It's a call to action to change the direction towards applying the diverse human potential to find the best solutions for the greater good of all.
> It's a call to action for an inclusive recovery and future.

To achieve this, we need to align our needs (current and future) to the types of talents and potential in the people that we are seeking. We need to attune to the ways that we reach out to attract talent, such as the position descriptions, the ways and places that we communicate about projects, initiatives, hiring, vacant positions, and the application and decision processes.

> We need to rethink about the people that we select, hire, and promote, and the ways that we do this. One thing that's for sure is the narrow profile and norms that have been dominating many talents selections in organisations and communities worldwide is the past.

The Great Reset extends to our talent selections in order to leverage the diverse human potential to co-create and build a fairer, more sustainable and resilient future.

As proven by numerous research studies for decades, diverse and inclusive teams and organisations have multiple advantages in performance, innovation, engagement, agility, creativity, user experience, and well-being as compare to homogeneous and non-inclusive organisations.[3] The same is true for inclusive communities where people are empowered to be societal actors with a joint vision for their community and society instead of passive recipients of public services or disempowered from having influence. Civic participation and inclusive development have the potential of significantly improving society along multiple dimensions, such as health and economy, when people feel included, autonomous, empowered, and socially connected. Moreover, helping to shape the decisions that affect our own life and the lives of other people is fundamental to human well-being. The benefits of inclusive organisations and societies at a larger scale are stability, higher transparency, lower corruption, a stronger rule of law, and higher trust in institutions and with each other.[4]

> We all have the power to reshape our future through the decisions that we make about people and the opportunities that we extend to people. By what we do, we can realise a collective goal for making inclusion the norm everywhere, for everyone.

## Why designing for inclusion is a must

But, making great talent selections and composing the best team of diversity does not happen by itself. Most evaluation and decision-making processes are designed based on a default and norm that favour a small and narrow segment of people and exclude rather than include a diverse segment of people and talent. It is a necessity that we make it a deliberate choice to design the evaluation and decision-making processes based on evidence how to de-bias each step in the process and make it inclusive by default. It is equally vital that the leadership and culture are inclusive [5] to leverage the human talent and potential of all people (see the *Action Guide for Leaders* with 30 Inclusion Nudges or *The Inclusion Nudges Guidebook* with 100 designs).

> To succeed with this, we need to address some hidden barriers and change some stuck patterns in our processes, systems, cultures, and behaviours. These challenges are not new and much effort has been done trying to solve them. At best these solutions are mostly ineffective, at worse these backlash, have slow progress, result in poor decisions, and leave us with some absurd realities.

In this Action Guide, we start by unfolding what we mean by this and then we give you 30 practical actions you can apply to fix this. Each Inclusion Nudge example is scripted out in detail how you can de-bias many of the process steps involved in talent attraction, selection, hiring, promotion, and composing teams. These will make inclusion the default and norm in your talent selection.

Let's begin by outlining some absurd realities that we need to change.

## A scenario based on reality

Imagine a group of leaders discussing a pool of qualified people for a senior management position. They just interviewed them and one of the leaders says,

*"The best qualified candidate is definitely the tallest of them.
No doubt. Tall leaders are the best at executing strategy.
Tall people have the most presence and are the most resilient in tough times.
They are the best leaders."*

And the human resource professional follows up on that view by stating,

*"Absolutely, our data shows the same. 60% of our executives are over 185 cm of height. Good choice. It doesn't matter that the shorter candidates have more merit and a better performance record."*

They all smile at each other. Job well done. They know they made the best choice about the best candidate for that leadership position. No doubt in their mind. But which mind?

## But which mind?

That is potentially the most important question you should be asking yourself right now. Let's take a look at why that is and how this book is going to make a critical difference in your talent processes and decision making moving forward.

Surely, no leaders who have the intention to hire the best qualified candidate, who perceive themselves to be a professional leader, and who know the cost of a recruitment process and the cost of hiring the wrong candidate, would *rationally* believe and consciously argue that tall people are the best leaders because they are tall. No, we wouldn't.

{ We don't do that with our conscious and rational mind.
So, the above scenario is absolutely absurd.
But the catch is that we do this with our unconscious and
instinctive mind, and thus, in our behaviours and decisions. }

We are all susceptible to this happening. And that turns this absurd scenario into an absurd reality. When left unaddressed, this absurd reality gets replicated time and time again in our organisations and communities. In this way, irrationality becomes our normative pattern.

Evidence from around the world and a wide body of research have proven over and over that height influences more heavily in decisions about leaders than their merit. This is a reality resulting in a population of top leaders where 60% of them are at or above 185 cm (6 ft 1 in) tall. On its own, perhaps this fact may not seem so absurd to you. But when compared to the general population, the irrationality emerges when knowing that only 14% of people have that height.[6]

This brings us back to the question about 'which mind?' and it also brings us to the purpose of leveraging the human potential of everyone and the diversity in our organisations and communities.

> How can we possibly succeed if we have such a profound and hidden gap between our rationality and our behaviour?
>
> What implications does this have when we select talent, hire, promote, compose our teams, and develop people?
>
> What is the impact on people, teams, projects, change, organisations, and communities?

SECTION 2

# Insights About the Human Mind

*Know the hidden barriers of the human mind and you will know exactly why you need to design for inclusive talent selection*

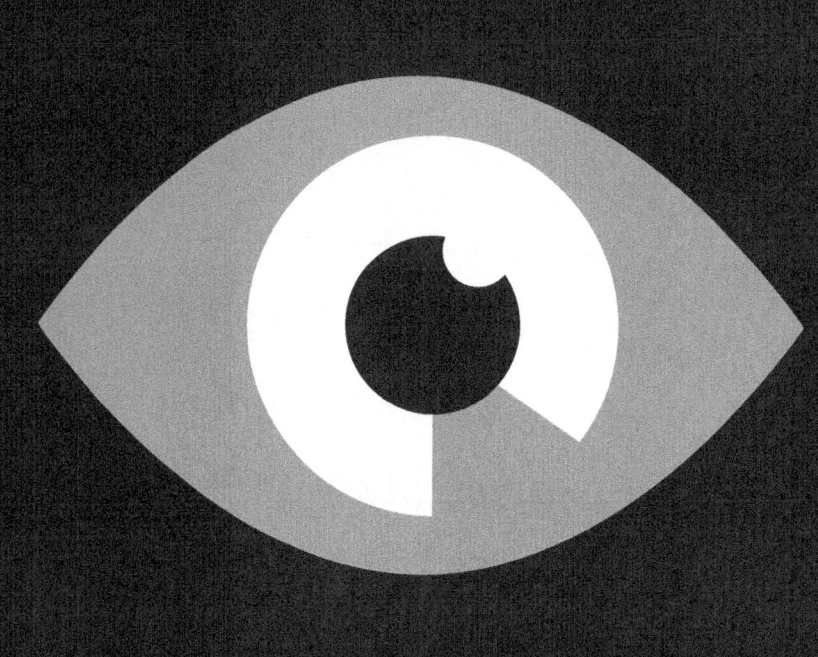

Insights About the Human Mind

The human mind is not one unified system of thinking. It has two inter-dependent modes of thinking. One is the unconscious, automatic system (1) and the other is the conscious, reflective system (2). See the distinction in the following illustration.

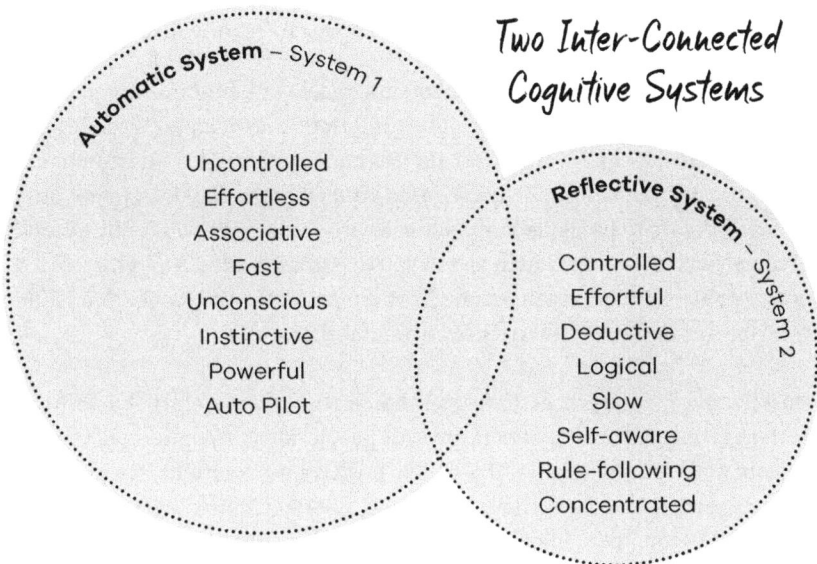

Image created by Christina Hucke, Lisa Kepinski and Tinna C. Nielsen based on works by Thaler, Sunstein, Haidt, Kahneman, and others

The majority of what we do and the decisions we make are based on instinctive and emotional reactions in our automatic system 1. This is a fast system, making split-second judgements and reactions, that we do not control.

{ The automatic system 1 is not really a system of **THINKING**, but more a system of **DOING**. }

> Our unconscious mind uses mental shortcuts, such as associations (perceived connection between elements or input) and biases (errors in processing and interpreting information or stimuli) to make judgements, to process, to make sense, to make choices, and to act.

These mental mechanisms and shortcuts enable our functioning to occur without using a lot of energy on interpretations and complex evaluations. Our reactions to the information and stimuli are effortless and automatic in the unconscious mind. In most cases, this works well, but in many other cases, errors in judgement and choices are made due to our split-second associations and biases, such as tall equals strong leader. And when faced with situations requiring mental effort due to ambiguity, complexity, and time-pressure, we rely even more on mental shortcuts.

Unreflective mental processes trigger thoughts, decisions, and behaviours in both negative and positive ways towards people, ideas, situations, language, objects, solutions, and more. If we have positive associations, we are more likely to process more of the information a person shares with us, or like their idea better, than when negative associations are triggered. We make a quick association between what we see or hear and a conclusion. The associations stemming from, for example, physical appearance will influence if we include or exclude people, information, and ideas. We also have an instinctive preference for the familiar and for similarity to ourselves and norms.

All of this will influence who we perceive as competent and likeable, and thus if we invite them for a job interview and what kind of questions we ask them. For example, as we've seen with the height example in deciding who to hire, promote, or vote for, none of this is registered in the conscious and self-reflective mind (system 2). This is because none of these snap perceptions and actions happen in the rational mode of thinking. In judgement and decision making, there is often a gap between system 1 and 2, between what we do and our intentions. The consequence is that we often behave or make choices that are against our own intentions, knowledge, and values. As a result, we are often blind to the negative implications that biases have on our behaviours and decisions.

Insights About the Human Mind

{ We are blind to the gap between our knowledge and intentions (system 2) to make the best talent selection decisions and have objective talent processes, while having behaviours and actions (system 1) that often result in selecting people based on irrelevant details steered by our unconscious instincts, associations, biases, and social dynamics. }

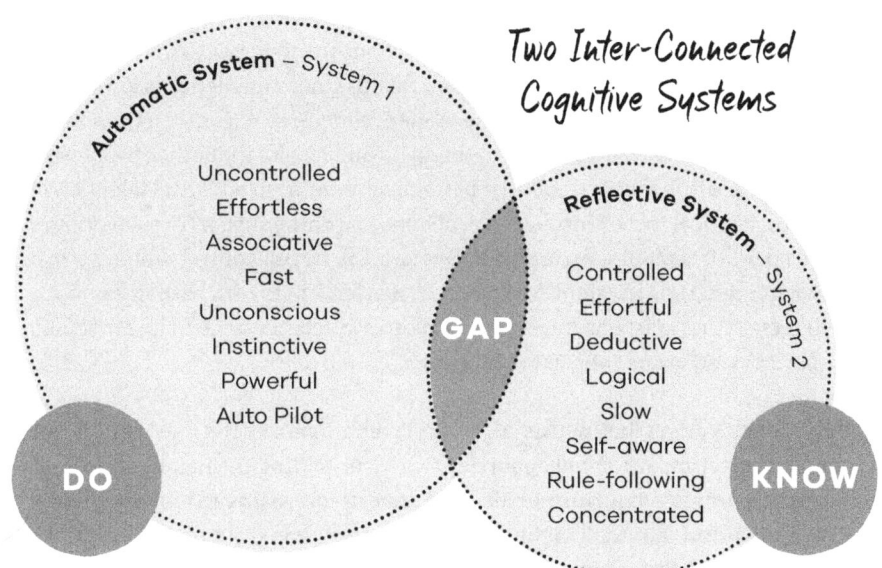

In the example of the height effect, this gap means that even when a hiring manager, HR professional, and citizen know in their rational mind that being tall does not guarantee you are a good leader or the best qualified, they still make a judgement and choice in their unconscious mind as if it did.

Research[7] shows that the unconscious mind has an instinctive and intuitive reaction based on associations (connections) between 'tall' and these characteristics ...

| | | |
|---|---|---|
| strong | impressive | attractive |
| powerful | persuasive | healthy |
| presence | convincing | capable |
| intelligent | highly motivated | effective |

These characteristics make our unconscious mind believe that the tallest person is the best leader and the best talent. Once that belief is activated, the rational mind searches for the evidence to prove it (confirmation bias). This is when we become blind to the facts and merits that other people (for instance, who are short) could be better leaders or high potential talents. We are susceptible to making flawed decisions and doing supporting behaviours based on this mental error (bias). System 1 is in full control when we use our 'gut reaction' in talent selections. When left on its own path in complex, diverse situations, our mind often makes poor choices due to unconscious instincts, emotions, and associations.

Let's take a closer look at this cognitive mechanism and the implications for talent selection and equal opportunities by unfolding the height effect and how it manifests as an unintended and undesirable reality in who we choose. Keep in mind that the height bias in just one example out of hundreds. We are unfolding this example to illustrate the complex, inherent systemic and mental barriers we can overcome by applying the Inclusion Nudges change approach.

### The height – leadership effect
In English, the word 'stature' has two meanings. The original definition simply means 'height'. While, the evolved, and more commonly-used, meaning is related to *"reputation and importance based on admirable qualities or achievements"*[8] and *"the amount of public respect or popularity that someone has"*.[9] It is in this latter context that the word 'stature' is often used to describe 'good leaders'. 'Stature' is also used to describe the people that we identify as 'great talents' in our organisations, governmental institutions, and communities.

The concept of 'stature' (also sometimes called 'presence') can be found in leadership and top talent ('high potentials') competency models, performance appraisals, biographies, job descriptions, and in writings on leadership and talent. The height-leadership effect is framed and reinforced by the use of this word which transcends from referencing physical measurement to describing desired traits and behaviours. *"The view that stature and leadership go hand in hand also permeates our language in expressions such as 'big men', 'oversee', 'look up to', and 'underling'."*[10] Even the phrase 'stand tall' reinforces 'courageous leadership', while we 'look down on' people we don't favour. Language reflects the absurd reality that we described at the beginning of this book.

This absurd reality is also seen in greater high-status opportunities available to tall people, with attaining higher education[11], more promotions, and higher incomes. Tall leaders' average earnings are 15% more than shorter leaders.[12] A large majority (86% of survey respondents) believe that height is an advantage in the workplace.[13] One way this shows up is employees not wanting to work for a short manager.[14]

The height-leadership effect is not just for business leaders. It also holds true for military leaders and political leaders in countries around the world. The heights are reflective of national averages, but the effect holds consistent. Tall leaders are the normative pattern. Local cultures do not mitigate this effect.

Perhaps you might be thinking,

> *"Surely, we humans are evolving in how we perceive competence and getting smarter with who we select as the most qualified?"*

Well, no. Research shows that rather than diminishing, the power of this height-leadership effect is actually increasing. For example, in the U.S., it's been over 100 years since a president was *"shorter than the average American male at that time, and since then, the average U.S. president has been 11.23 cm (4.42 in) taller than the average American male"*.[15] There are world leaders height indexes[16] also showing this effect globally.

Height is registered in our mind as a desired trait. One survey found that 45% of men 172 cm (5 ft 8 in) or under wished they were taller.[17] This wish can become a false self-belief. When we feel powerful, we tend to believe we are taller than we actually are.[18] There is a boost in confidence that comes from just feeling tall, influencing performance and being more likely to go for leadership roles.[19] So that's how we may feel, but what about how we see others? Well, that also has an effect. Leaders who are perceived as powerful are estimated by other people to be taller than they really are.[20] This connection of powerful leader and height fools us into believing something not true in reality—about ourselves and about others.

You might be thinking, *"What?! How silly!!"* But guess what? This association of power and tall can take us even further with great steps to carry out the illusion of height to enhance how we feel and how others may see and respond to us.

There is a careful art to trying to appear taller, such as with shoes with higher soles, fluffy hair styles, and clothing. The environment for leaders is also adjusted to increase a sense of height. Think of a group of political leaders speaking at podiums, such as a press briefing. There is great care that goes into using standing platforms to create the appearance of equal height. Height diplomacy is also called upon when orchestrating group photos and the placement of leaders relative to size. Height perception for a politician equates to power. And this is similarly played out in many organisations with group photos of senior leaders. The height effect is also amplified by the angle of the camera to elongate the body, with the 'tall' photos appearing in political ads, in organisational reports, media, photos on the walls in organisations, and resumes. Seeing is believing, and great care is taken to show height however possible.

Going beyond pretending to be taller, this desire has led to a new form of invasive cosmetic surgery. Legs are lengthened by breaking bones and inserting bars and screws to gain a few centimetres of height. Across many countries, this business often plays on the insecurities of being short and the link to career and personal opportunities due to height.[21]

The height effect can be manifested with harassing behaviours. Some politicians have openly ridiculed their opponents' shorter statures in an attempt to increase their own political advantage.[22] It has been raised that bullying and discrimination of short men ('heightism') should be part of inclusion and equity initiatives.[23]

### Clearly, there is a preference for tall people, but does it benefit *all* tall people?

Well, no, not exactly. Research shows that height is not a benefit for everyone. The height advantages most predominately benefit light skin-tone men and not darker skin-tone men nor women of any skin tone.[24] Height for these people can carry less of a reward, often with serious penalty.

For tall Black and Brown men, cognitive associations of 'threat' and 'danger' can be activated in the minds of White people, triggering emotions of 'discomfort' and 'fear'. This shapes behaviour, with more adverse, discriminatory impact. For example, research has shown that in the U.S. tall Black and Brown men who are 193 cm (6 ft 4 in) or taller are 6.2 times more likely to be stopped by the police as compared to a White man of the same height.[25] Also, tall men of colour are frequently assumed (based on snap judgements, stereotypes, and social categorisation) to be basketball players (no other professions) and also to not have high intelligence and other talents. Amongst peers of Black and Brown tall men, how their talents are described varies by skin tone, with the darker the skin, the less focus on their performance and abilities, but instead on their physical appearance.[26] However, within 'professional contexts' there can be career benefits to tall men of colour, but not to the same degree of White men.[27] For example, the darker the skin colour, the lower the pay to tall men.[28] The height effect for Black and Brown men is not as strong as for White men, and even can lead to life and career limitations. Tall Black and Brown men have dual implications of 'tall' in society (discriminating against them) and in a professional context (somewhat favouring them).

For women, tall height prompts associations of being 'odd'. They don't fit implicit femininity norms ('what women should look like'). This can be the source of social biases against tall women. In the reality of a lack of gender parity in workplaces and society, *"The typical chief executive is six feet tall with a deep voice—a typical woman doesn't match the image."*[29] Yet still, the height effect does seem to still hold for women in work to some degree. For instance, there are very few CEO and top leadership positions held by women, but of these many women leaders were still above the height average for women overall.[30] Another study found that against the context of the existing gender and race wage gaps, there were still some increased earning benefits for all tall woman (of colour and White), but not as much as for White men.[31]

So, the height-leadership effect is predominately benefiting white men, who are usually the majority in leadership roles, with some smaller benefits to other tall people. The tall effect has a 'first class' and 'second class' tiered impact reflecting our inequitable society.

## Absurd realities
## Our beliefs?

Surely, with our rational mind, we do not believe that …

- Light skin-tone tall men are more skilled than their height counterparts who have darker skin tones or are women

- The tallest people are more skilled due to their height and should be appointed to be leaders

- All short people must follow tall people

- Tall people are smarter and therefore make better students

- We should vote for tall political leaders and prime ministers because they will be the best at leading the country since they are tall and have long legs

- Tall people should be paid more based on their height, and even given a bonus for every centimetre (inch) taller they are as compared to other people

- Society is better off with only tall people in charge

- We are safer with lighter skin tone tall people than darker skin tone tall people

- Outside of work, 'tall' is 'good' for White men, but 'tall' is 'bad' for Black and Brown men and they should be punished more for their height; and that punishment should be incrementally increased based on their height

> Even when we don't believe this with our rational mind, evidence still shows that we evaluate and make choices (hire, select, develop, assess, promote, pay, vote) as if we do believe this.
> The intention-action gap holds us back from making objective, merit-based talent selections.

Let's take a closer look at this gap and blind spots and unfold how these play out in talent selection in multiple and often unimaginable ways, and manifest as an unintended and undesirable realities.

## Absurd realities
## Many implications of our unconscious actions

A body of research, as well as evidence from organisations and communities worldwide, show the implications of our unconscious actions and the resulting absurdities that play out.

> As you read this, please stay optimistic.
> We have made sure that the 30 inclusive actions in this Action Guide empower you to change these and make inclusion the norm everywhere, for everyone.

## Accent matters

### Reality!
It takes us less than 30 seconds to linguistically profile a speaker and make quick decisions on their ethnic origin, socio-economic class, and their backgrounds. We are more likely to be biased against people who have accents different to ours or are markers for undesirable characteristics that we unconsciously attribute to certain accents. We assign values, such as pleasantness and prestige but also intelligence, based on accent. A non-native accent is also a proven barrier to career progression and access to entrepreneurial investment. Furthermore, we (unconsciously) believe more in facts shared with us by a person who has the same accent as ourselves, than when those same facts are shared with us by a person with an unfamiliar accent.[32]

### Absurd?
Surely no one would say that they hire someone based on their accent? Or that they discount what is said by a colleague who has an accent different from their own? But in our behaviour, this is a reality and the implications are manifold.

### Your actions?
→ Are you wondering about how your talent assessments and selection decisions may have been affected by the accents of the people that you interacted with?
→ Are you wondering about how others view you based on your own accent?

## Identity questions matter

### Reality!
People underperform on skills assessments when they answer questions about their age, gender, ethnicity, race, physical abilities, and income right before doing a test. This is because they internalise the negative associations and stereotypes of their identity groups (called stereotype threat). An example is when having to register gender before a math test, this influences women and girls to underperform because they internalise the stereotype that they are 'bad at math' despite their abilities being the same as, or more skilled than, men and boys. Similarly, it influences performance when perceived stronger groups are in the test group. In the U.S., White men who felt strong at math actually performed worse when learning before a test that their results would be compared with Asian-American men who were believed to be better at math. There can be a boost of positive results when the stereotype is positive, such as 'men are good at computers' (called stereotype uplift) or when priming for a perceived positive identity aspect.[33]

### Absurd?
People do not believe with their rational mind that 'neutral' information (such as age, nationality, gender, race/ethnicity, etc.) can activate a stereotype so strongly in themselves nor that it can influence their abilities and self-efficacy. And we don't believe that about others. If we did know this, we would be more deliberate about what information we ask for or tell people, and when we do that.

### Your actions?
→ Are you wondering about an assessment that you conducted or relied upon the results for a talent decision? Are you wondering about how valid it was? If the order of the questions may have caused errors? Or could people have underperformed based on stereotype activation that your assessment triggered rather than their actual abilities??

→ Who are you missing out on? What kind of profiles are you deselecting?

# Recent doing matters

### Reality!

What happened most recently will influence how and what we remember over a longer period. If the most recent experience was positive, then that will have a positive spill-over effect on all the other things that happened. Or if the last experience was negative, then that can make us remember all the previous elements in that event or period as negative, even though we experienced them as positive at the time that they happened.

This recency bias and memory bias also influences decision-making and assessments in investment, social welfare, future planning, innovation, and basically in all other contexts as well. It has also been proven to impact on employee performance evaluations because we tend to assess the most recent episode in performance, while (unintentionally) ignoring all other work done over the full evaluation time. This skews the performance assessment comments and the resulting rating (and related compensation) and will have implications for the person's access to opportunities. Due to memory bias, we cannot remember our own perception of what people do over a period. The only way is to note down after every incidence or task solved how we viewed each performance. Then when making the collected evaluation, we have what we need to avoid the recency bias.

### Absurd?

No professional leader wants to make evaluations and decisions based only on a fraction of the relevant information or data available. But it turns out, that's what we do on a regular basis when we have not designed our processes to make sure all elements are included.

### Your actions?
→ Are you wondering about lost opportunities and flawed evaluations of people and their performance because what happened most recently?
→ Are you wondering how this might have and will influence who is promoted or selected for a project?

## Names matters

### Reality!

Names influence how we perceive people and connote personality characteristics and also determine how competent we perceive people to be. More than 1000 CV studies[34] have shown that the same CV with different names, immigrant status, schools, number of children, photos, and other identity data, that were sent to actual positions advertised (matched with qualifications) were rated completely different due to these diversity dimensions. When it comes to the name, the discrimination was profound. Across all countries in the study, there was a preference for 'traditional' names. In the U.S, 'White' names received 50% more call backs for interviews than 'African-American' names.[35] A similar pattern was found in France for 'French' names and 'North African' names.[36] In the UK, people with 'Middle Eastern' names had to make 80% more applications than 'British names'.[37]

We would like to think that bias triggered by a name at least disappears when we know the person and can evaluate them based on their merit. Evidence shows another reality. We form more positive impressions of people with easy-to-pronounce names than of difficult-to-pronounce names. Some implications are that people with easier-to-pronounce names occupy higher status positions. We promote people more quickly and we vote for people with names that we find easy. We also believe more in statements from people with familiar names.[38]

### Absurd?

Who would deliberately and rationally select people for work that we consider important based on how easy it is to say their name? No one hopefully, but most do unconsciously.

### Your actions?
→ Are you wondering if you have de-selected the best qualified person due to their name?
→ Are you wondering if you have offered opportunities to people that you feel comfortable with because their name is easy to pronounce?

## Speaking first matters

### Reality!

If a person with high authority opens a discussion with their view, then others can hold back from offering contrary important information, and go along with the prevailing view and perhaps incorrect information, due to an unconscious belief that 'status' equates to the 'correct' view. The first people speaking up in a group will also influence the perception and engagement of others in the group. Unconsciously, our perceptions are influenced by people, but also consciously because we have an innate social need to be accepted by the group. This means that we adjust our view and conform to the majority view and social norms. The consequences are that we neither have access to the diversity of knowledge, perspectives and skills in the group, nor leverage the benefit of diversity. Furthermore, group conformity and self-silencing have proven to increase the risk of errors in problem solving and decision making.[39]

### Absurd?

Have you met leaders or project managers saying that they always speak first themselves or let the most powerful in the group speak first with the intention to make everyone else in the group contribute less, self-silence, or doubt their own view and thus not share it?

We haven't! But we have seen it play out in almost all teams again and again. And research supports this.

### Your actions?
→ Are you wondering if you are getting access to the diversity of attributes and skills in meetings (including interviews, hiring panel selection meetings, performance reviews, and more) that you facilitate? If you are missing out on new opportunities or wasting potential?
→ Are you wondering if your talent selection processes might be steered simply by who speaks first?

## Gender matters

### Reality!

Studies show the same behaviour is evaluated differently by gender. When people are shown pictures of crying baby girls and asked, *"What feeling is the baby girl expressing?"*, the majority say *"anxiety"*. But when the same photos are positioned as boys, then the babies are perceived as *"angry"*.[40] A professor[41] conducted an experiment using a case study on the successful entrepreneur and venture capitalist Heidi Roizen. In the experiment, two versions of the case study were created. Everything was the same in both, except in one version the name was changed from Heidi to Howard. A group of MBA students rated the original Heidi version and another group rated the Howard version. They answered questions such as *"Would you make the same choices as her/him to succeed?", "Would you want her/him as a mentor ... go out for a beer with ... collaborate with .... work for ...."*. The only similarity in their rating of the Heidi and Howard versions was that they found Heidi and Howard equally competent. But Heidi was perceived as too assertive, too aggressive, too selfish, and they would not seek her out for collaboration nor hire her. But with Howard, well, they loved him! And this was the case for ratings by both the men and women. A Norwegian study used the names of Hanna and Hans, and the results were similar.[42]

### Absurd?

Who would de-select and 'punish' powerful and successful women because they don't behave in alignment with the stereotypical perception of how a woman is 'supposed to behave' and because they behave exactly in alignment with the masculine-coded performance norm? Would that confuse us because women are not men? No, we don't think so, right? Determining good performance is objective and not genderised, right? But it does confuse the unconscious mind when women do not play by the feminine norms but instead by the masculine norms – and the opposite is true for men.

### Your Action?

→ Are you wondering if you are also perceiving competent and ambitious women as 'too assertive while at the same expecting that of a man? Are you wondering what the implications this has on your behaviour and talent decisions?

## Children matter

### Reality!
Studies show that women who were identified as not having children received 2.1 more call backs for interviews than women who were identified as mothers. But for women in their 30's and who don't have children, hiring biases prevailed based on the belief that they may become pregnant. While in talent selection decisions, men who are fathers are perceived as better qualified than women who are mothers. For most men, the fact of fatherhood results in a wage bonus, while for most women, motherhood results in a wage penalty and this increases with each child they have.[43] Other studies have found that the largest fatherhood earning bonuses went to men who are White, married, in households with a traditional gender division of labour, are college graduates, in a professional or managerial role, and whose jobs emphasise cognitive skills and deemphasise physical strength. They received more than other men who are also fathers but do not match these characteristics of stereotypical masculinity within the majority of workplaces. And to help meet the needs of being a working parent, men were much more likely (70%) to be granted a flexible work option than women (57%) when positioned as a need for child-care reasons, and women were 4 times more seen as not committed to work.[44]

### Absurd?
Why would fathers be perceived as more committed to their work and careers but mothers be perceived as the opposite? Why would working mothers be seen as less competent and less warm (likeable) than working fathers? Why would women's fertility be a factor in talent decisions? Why would it not be assumed that women are as likely as men to be the main income earner (the 'breadwinner') for the family?

### Your actions?
→ Are you wondering about how 'caregiver' stereotypes may have unduly influenced your talent decisions for both men and women, parents and those without children?
→ Wondering how this may have contributed to a gender pay gap?
→ Are you curious if there is equity in who can work from home without career limiting implications?

## Work allocation matters

**Reality!**

Perceived low value tasks ('office housekeeping tasks') are much more assigned to minorities and women on the team, while high visibility projects go to 'star' performers. These 'top' talents often mirror the majority norms in the organisation; they 'fit in' and as a result we may notice them more favourably. They are top of mind when there is a good opportunity for development and we trust them more to do it. It becomes a reinforcing cycle and confirmation bias kicks in to justify entrusting the 'star' performers with the top priority projects. This unequal allocation of work across the team is often influenced by stereotypes and social categorisation, and we are often blind to this happening. Women and minorities are perceived, and often behave accordingly, that they 'should take on' these roles. There can be group dynamics and peer pressure for them to do these, even to the point that they volunteer more to do them. These types of tasks are typically 'on top of the day job', and so carry an extra work load. When performance evaluations occur, it's the high visibility projects that are recalled and praised. These are 'career bonus' opportunities, with the potential to accelerate promotions. While the low value tasks take time away from core work and go without recognition, thus creating a penalty situation.[45]

**Absurd?**

Why would we ask, but not recognise and reward work such as organising events, serving on committees, maybe even a diversity council, etc.? Why would we not equally share work across all on the team?

**Your actions?**
- Are you wondering if there is a inequality in the division of labour based on skin tone, race, ethnicity, and/or gender?
- Are you wondering if you have made a talent decision to rule someone out due to them having 'team-supporting' tasks on their resume, and this made you to think less of their potential?
- Wondering if someone's talents and performance have been over-exhausted due to extra 'team-housekeeping' work having to be done in addition to their core, daily work?

These unconscious biases and behaviours are just a small selection of examples of the absurd realities that we are all create with our actions and without having intentions to do so. These illustrations of the implications of how biases can de-rail our behaviour and cultures are a reminder of the importance of being inclusive in how we do talent selections.

If you want to learn more about how you are influenced by mental shortcuts and unconscious associations in talent selection, we recommend you to take some of the many Implicit Association Tests: https://implicit.harvard.edu/implicit/

But don't stop with that. And don't get despondent in realising your biases. We all have these. Instead, use the insights you gained about your own quick associations to energise you in taking action to be inclusive. You have 30 actions you can do in this book.

It's the 'doing' that we need to focus most on to close the intention-action gap.

With your rational mind, you might be thinking that as civilised human beings we are evolving and getting smarter. But that's not the case.

## Exclusion is not diminishing

Research shows that rather than diminishing, progress is very slow or stalled.[46] In many cases, exclusion is increasing. In the workplace, one large study found that 40% of U.S. employees felt excluded.[47] While another study across 4 countries found that discrimination was experienced or witnessed by 55% of U.K. employees, 43% of French employees, 37% of German employees, and 61% of U.S. employees. And across all 4 countries, half of the employees felt their organisations should take more action to increase inclusion, equity, and diversity.[48] A body of research shows that rather than diminishing, the power of the unconscious mind is actually increasing due to cognitive overload as a result of increased complexity and social media echo-chambers of homogeneity, and increasingly busy and stressed lives. All of which intensifies our need for mental shortcuts and effortless judgement and choices. This results in greater homogeneity and exclusion at the expense of our collective need for inclusion of diversity in our organisations and communities.

{ We are beyond inclusion being 'nice to have'.
Inclusion is a global and local necessity.
The need for inclusive talent selection
and creating inclusive cultures is growing. }

The question is how to transform the current state to a more inclusive norm – everywhere, for everyone. And how, with your courageous talent decisions and processes, this can happen.

SECTION 3

# How to Change Absurd Realities to Great Talent Selection

> Awareness about hidden barriers and unconscious bias is not the solution — designing for inclusion is

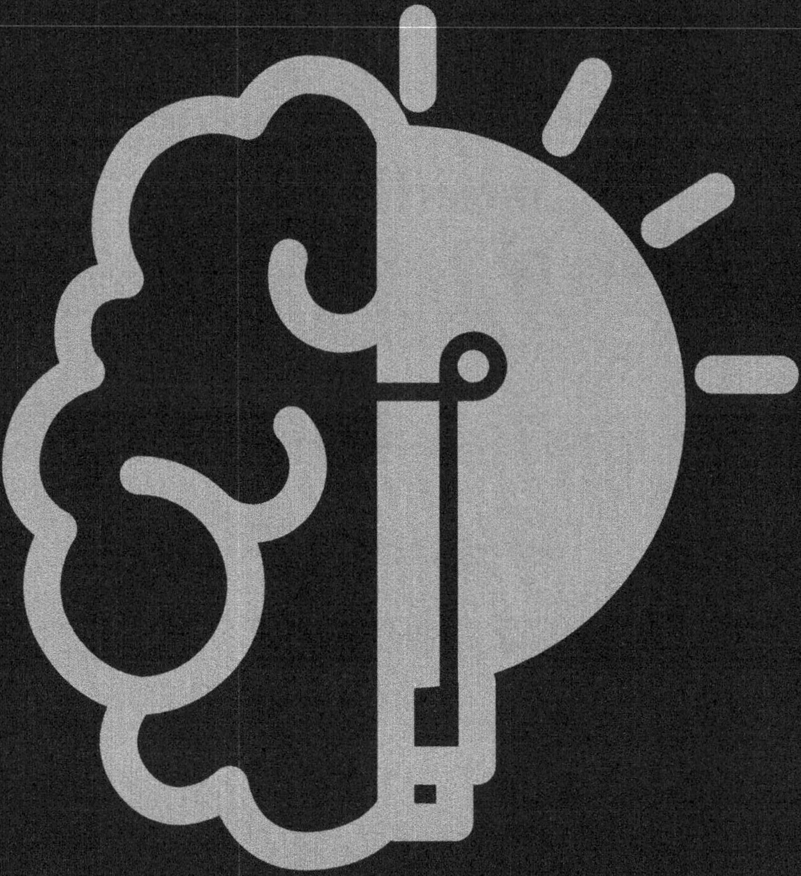

We cannot change and redesign how the human mind works. Knowing about our cognitive biases and the gap between the two systems in our mind, will not change how it influences us. And trying to be consciously aware of the unconscious while evaluating and making decisions about people, talents and potential, is going to give us cognitive overload that will do the opposite of changing it.

> What works is applying behavioural insights to close the gap between our two cognitive systems.
> By design, we can change the barriers of the mind into strengths.

### Bias awareness is not the solution

Unfortunately, many tend to think that unconscious bias awareness (training) is the solution. But, we cannot with willpower and good intentions in the rational mind change the automatic reactions in the unconscious mind. Research and real experiences are showing that unconscious bias awareness training can even backfire because it unintentionally enhances more biased thinking and behaviours, as well as strengthens stereotypes.

Also, by hearing that others are biased and its 'natural' to hold biases and stereotypes, we feel less motivated to change these. Even worse, by attending such trainings, it can create a self-perception of having control of ones' biases and being one of the 'good people' not discriminating. This has proven to trigger moral licensing,[49] which makes our behaviour not only non-inclusive, but the very opposite of our stated values, beliefs, and intentions. Moral licensing is an unconscious mental phenomenon in which a positive self-image makes our unconscious mind more likely to make immoral choices. Studies[50] have shown that people who have expressed strong disagreement with sexist statements are more likely to hire a man for a job and make sexist comments because they (unconsciously) feel secure about their 'non-sexist' self-image. People who express disagreement with racist statements have also been shown to be more likely to unconsciously discriminate against racial minorities.

We might think we are motivated by our sense of ethics, but we are not. The problem is that once we believe we are ethical, we unconsciously care less about actually behaving ethically as well as past good behaviour makes us 'sinners'.[51]

{ This might sound absurd. Moral licensing is absurd. Your first reaction might be, "I don't do that!". But the evidence is so conclusive that it is more absurd to believe we are exempt from having the same cognitive mechanisms as everyone else. }

The global trend of offering unconscious bias training is an expression of hope that these sessions will somehow 'fix' our biased thinking, interactions, and processes. We, the authors, do acknowledge that such sessions can create a shared experience and aha-moments, and thus create a shared language that can make it easier to collectively address or call out bias during the talent selection process. But these types of awareness trainings are not the magic solution for mitigating bias and promoting more inclusive evaluations and decisions about talents.

{ We are talking to the wrong brain system and we are speaking the wrong language. }

Perhaps you might now be thinking, "What can we do about this?". Well, fortunately there are proven ways to address this in an effective way to make change happen in our talent processes and decision-making. See the following list of what is proven to work.

### What is proven to work:

→ **Evidenced-based.** Get the full picture by measuring and reviewing data to reveal what's really happening across all stages in your talent selection process. Be informed, rather than using guess work (which is often biased) or copying so-called 'best practices' done by others. Use your own data to know your situation—both successes and challenges. Then, you can take targeted action by applying the needed process designs that are specific to your context.

→ **Process design.** Tweak, adjust, change, and redesign each step in the talent selection processes to mitigate the influence of bias. Make sure you and your peers evaluate and assess people and merit as objectively as possible, and make inclusive judgements and decisions. Make sure the talent selection process is designed to help close the gaps between intentions and outcomes.

→ **Measure & share.** Applying behavioural designs is not an exact science. You must adapt actions to your context, then apply, and measure the outcomes. Redesign if needed, and share with others so they can learn from the experience. Spark a wider change initiative.

→ **Facilitation.** Make sure the way evaluations, discussions, meetings, collaboration, and decision making in groups are facilitated is designed to reduce group conformity, biases, self-silencing, and are inclusive.

→ **Micro-strategies.** Use micro-strategies to change your micro-behaviour in your interaction with other people in the selection committee, hiring team, project group, candidate interview. Make sure your unconscious mind does not influence you to listen less to some people, ask more questions to others, use micro-gestures with some and not with others, and ensure you give all equal opportunities to be at their very best.

This Action Guide as well as the other Action Guides in this series, are about doing exactly that. You get 30 examples of Inclusion Nudges to make it easy for you to do inclusion as the norm in decision making and in all talent selection processes. You can make it happen!

SECTION 4:

# The Power of the Inclusion Nudges Change Approach

*How applying behavioural insights and inclusive design makes a significant difference*

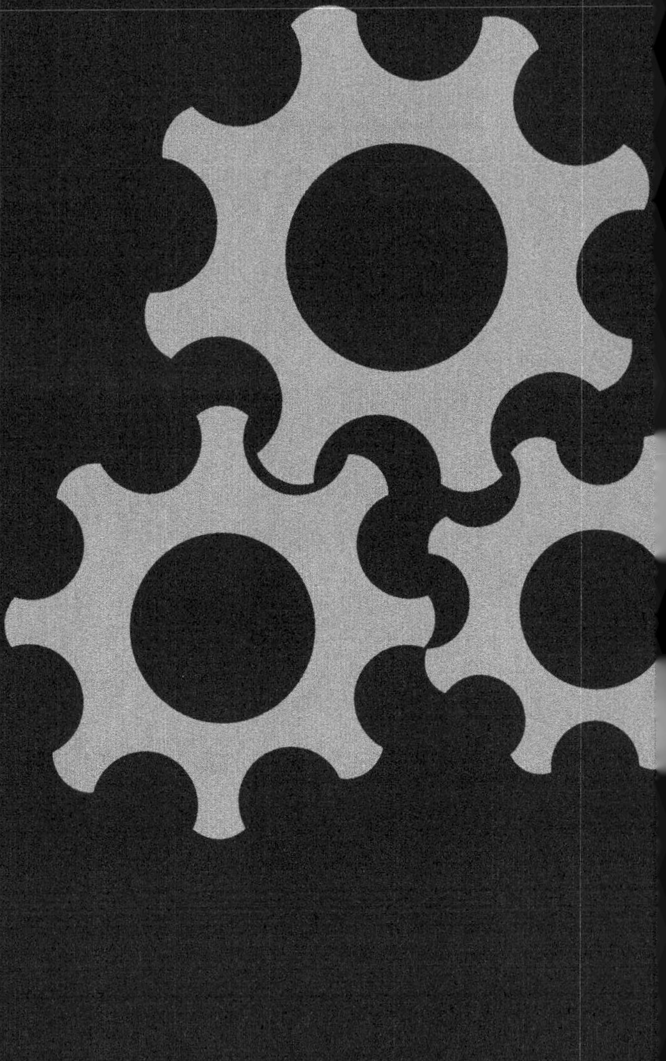

## What is an Inclusion Nudge?

Okay, now it's time to dig into the Inclusion Nudges change approach and understand what an Inclusion Nudge is and how it works. The inclusive actions in this Action Guide are grounded in the evidence-based change approach called Inclusion Nudges.

> An **INCLUSION NUDGE** is an action designed to influence the unconscious mind and makes it easy to be inclusive and do inclusion automatically in daily actions.
>
> These actions are practical applications of basic insights about human behaviour and decision making (from behavioural and social sciences, nudge theory, as well as knowledge about the hidden barriers to achieve inclusion). These inclusive actions work because they nudge (steer) the unconscious mind (your own and that of others) to change behaviour to be inclusive in alignment with our knowledge about the importance of this and also in alignment with our own intentions to make great talent selections.

The Inclusion Nudges change approach has three purposes and, thus, three types of designed actions that work – sometimes separately and sometimes together. These are described below.

### Three types of Inclusion Nudges

→ **Process actions:** You can design processes to ensure the ability in yourself and in others to be and do inclusion automatically in daily actions. Research has identified that change comes from making it effortless to do the new behaviour. That's why it's crucial and effective to design processes (meeting facilitation, decision making, idea generation, innovation, promotions, hiring, strategy planning, and more) in ways that reduce the negative influence of bias and are inclusive of diverse perspectives by default. This is an effective way to engage people in making the culture in teams, communities, and organisations inclusive as the norm. We call these *Process Design* Inclusion Nudges.

→ **Framing actions:** You can change your own perceptions and split-second judgements, as well as those of other people by the words you use, the way you communicate, how you present a problem, issue, task, or set up the physical space. A body of research shows how our perceptions are influenced by hidden cues that trigger associations in our unconscious mind. When you change the cues, you can prime action, and change perceptions of diversity as a 'burden' to be a 'resource', you can mitigate and change negative stereotypes, perceptions, and also increase individual performance. We call these *Framing Perceptions* Inclusion Nudges.

→ **Motivational actions:** You visualise the hidden patterns and the implications of these both to yourself and to others to create motivation in the unconscious mind to be inclusive. You can get many people engaged in creating the changes without having to tell them to or convince them. Research has proven again and again that change happens when we see and feel the need for change (in the unconscious mind) and not when we rationally understand the need for change. We call these *Feel the Need* Inclusion Nudges.

The actions in this book are a mix of process actions and framing actions.

In *The Inclusion Nudges Guidebook* and the *Action Guide for Motivating Allies* you get many examples of the motivational actions (*Feel the Need* Inclusion Nudges).

## Thought leaders for a new approach

The Inclusion Nudges change approach was developed by the authors, Lisa Kepinski and Tinna C. Nielsen, in 2013 when we were both working as leaders with global responsibility for inclusion and diversity internally in multinationals – Lisa in France and Tinna in Denmark. We merged our change approaches and backgrounds in behavioural sciences, as well as our experience as leaders and change makers, and we developed the concept and coined the term 'Inclusion Nudges'. Today, Inclusion Nudges is internationally recognised as game changing and as a means to achieve inclusive outcomes effectively.

We partner with some of the biggest public and private corporations in the world, universities, municipalities, community groups, city developers and architects, social activists, and the United Nations, to redesign their talent selection processes with the focus of mitigating the influence of bias, stereotypes, implicit norms, discrimination, and design each step of the processes to be as inclusive as possible. We have done this by designing and applying Inclusion Nudges, we have experimented, and we have shared what works and doesn't work to inspire, just like we have been inspired by others.

The Inclusion Nudges change approach is inspired by behavioural economics and the nudge theory created by Nobel Laurate Richard Thaler and Cass Sunstein. Nudging is a technique that helps people change their behaviour without the need of convincing them with rational arguments, threats, or punishments. A nudge is choice architecture, where the environment, the system default, or the anchor of the thought process has been designed to help the unconscious mind automatically make a directed choice in a predictable direction.[52] The person does not think actively about the change nor do they need to engage their own willpower to alter behaviour. Thaler and Sunstein describe a good nudge as a behavioural intervention that is carried out to influence the choice and behaviour of people in accordance with their own interests or good intentions.

## The power of nudging and Inclusion Nudges

Both nudging and Inclusion Nudges have these commonalities:

- Minimising the impact of mental shortcuts
- Not relying on the conscious mind to drive change
- Not using rational arguments to convince people to change
- Making the desired behaviour automatic
- Align behaviour with self-interest and intent
- Not using threats or punishment
- Respecting freedom of choice
- Mostly low cost or no cost
- Nudging for the greater good

The Inclusion Nudges change approach closes the gaps and makes it easy to *do* inclusiveness as the norm everywhere. The power of this approach is that you are not the one pushing and pulling for this to happen. With this change approach the changes are driven and owned by all the people involved in the talent selection process.

{ The most powerful about this approach is the potential of turning the barriers of the unconscious mind into strengths and levers for inclusive change, business, growth, and development. }

## Intentional and inclusive choice architecture

Everything around us is *'choice architecture'* which is influencing our decisions and behaviour. We should make sure that our talent selection, as well as organisations, communities, policies, and society are actually designed with intentional choice architecture that will be good for people and will be inclusive. This was our motivation back in 2013 for merging our extensive knowledge about inclusion, diversity, and equality with nudge theory to create the Inclusion Nudges change approach and global initiative.

{ Inclusion is the core of strong and successful organisations and communities. Being inclusive of all talents is vital to achieve this. }

We published the 3rd edition of *The Inclusion Nudges Guidebook* (2020) with 100 examples to empower and enable as many people as possible to make inclusion the norm everywhere, for everyone. This Action Guide contains 30 examples that have been specifically selected for talent selection situations. To get more inspiration and examples, we encourage you to read the full guidebook to get the 100+ examples and/or the other books in the Inclusion Nudges Action Guide Series.

Also, take a look at the Inclusion Nudges global initiative website for many more resources to support you leading inclusively.
www.inclusion-nudges.org

## The Definitions We Use

To set the guiding frame, here is a model that we, Lisa Kepinski and Tinna C. Nielsen, have created based on decades of working with communities, organisations, teams, leaders, human resource departments and recruitment professionals across many sectors. It gives an overview of the many components of inclusive actions.

The Inclusion Nudges examples in this Action Guide are relevant across all of the **INCLUSIVE** Action Model elements (see next page). This will make it easy for you to make sure you cover all the aspects of inclusive talent selections.

Turn the page to see how we define inclusive actions.

## The INCLUSIVE Action Model

**I** — Include people, information, ideas, & knowledge instead of exclude

**N** — Nurture & embrace differences with empathy instead of polarising

**C** — Conquer outdated social norms & discriminatory practices instead of maintaining them

**L** — Leverage diversity of perspectives & backgrounds instead of under-utilising people's abilities & the mix

**U** — Undermine the negative impact of unconscious biases instead of focusing on awareness

**S** — Seek out diversity instead of homogeneity

**I** — Implement redesigns of practices, processes, & systems based on facts & behavioural insights

**V** — Verbalise support & actions for inclusion, diversity, & equality instead of silent consent

**E** — Empower people and groups instead of disempower

*The INCLUSIVE Action Model developed by Inclusion Nudges Founders, Tinna C. Nielsen & Lisa Kepinski, © 2020*

## Diversity: The mix of all of us
Diversity is about people. This includes their demographic differences, backgrounds, multiple identities, and their unique experiences, perspectives, knowledge, abilities, ideas, and more. Diversity is not referencing specific characteristics of only 'the minority' within a group of people or in society. Diversity is referencing all people and differences among us. Diversity is the mix of all of us.

## Equity: The fairness frame for the mix
Equity is about ensuring that all people have equal access to opportunities and fair treatment, and ensuring elimination of discriminatory practices, systems, laws, policies, social norms, and cultural traditions. Equity encompasses a balancing of power and correcting where inequality exists. It is also about patterns of behaviour and processes developed and used which may be continuing inequality. Within some contexts, equity may have a legal mandate attached to achieving it, along with penalties for not. The intent of equity is fairness to all.

## Inclusion: Welcoming and applying the mix
Inclusion is focused on fostering the structure, system, processes, culture, behaviour, and mindset that embrace and respect all people and all our diversity. It embraces all people. Inclusion is about ensuring that diversity of knowledge, perspectives, information, and ideas are welcomed and being used. Inclusion is when we seek out diversity, when we challenge excluding norms and stereotypes, when we are open to others, and when we speak up. Inclusion is when all people are valued and able to participate and contribute to their fullest. Inclusion is welcoming and applying the mix of all of us.

## Belonging: I feel valued as a part of the mix
Belonging focuses on the person's experience within a setting—they are welcomed, structures exist to ensure fairness, and they feel that they can be their full, authentic self within that culture, group, or setting. They don't have to cover who they are or downplay personal traits. As a result, they don't suffer the limiting toll this can bring. Belonging is when people feel seen and heard, feel they naturally belong to a group, feel safe, and feel valued. This results from having equitable and inclusive practices, norms, cultures, and systems. When diversity, equity, and inclusion are done well, then belonging results.

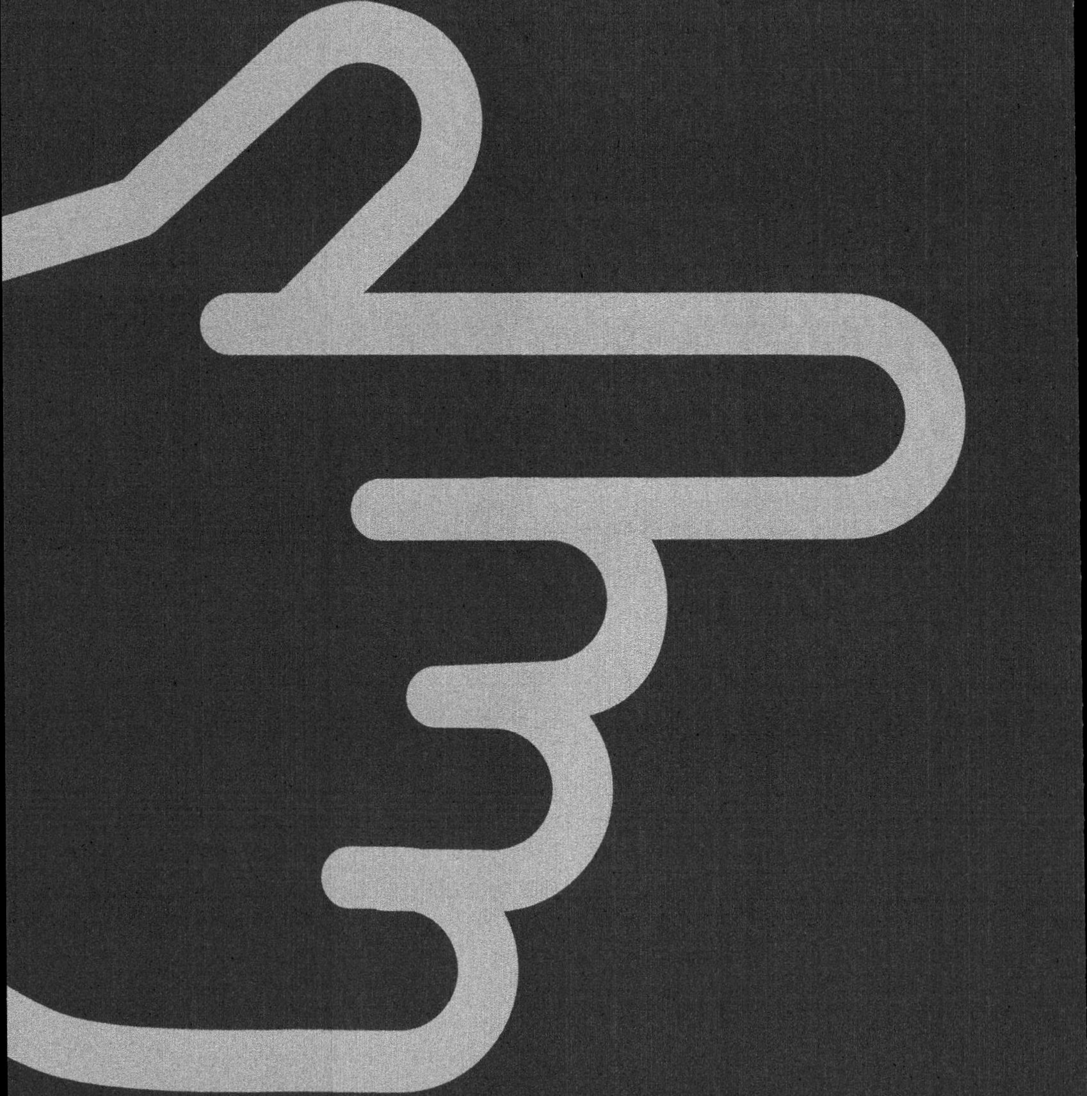

SECTION 5

# Inclusive Actions for Talent Selection

> Action by action,
> I make
> inclusion the norm –
> everywhere, for everyone

## How to use this Action Guide

This Action Guide offers you 30 practical examples (Inclusion Nudges) to be inclusive in your work to achieve better outcomes with talent selection. These are mapped out against some of the talent selection process steps. Inclusion Nudges are designs that contribute to mitigating the influence of unconscious bias and making processes inclusive by default and as the norm.

The examples will spark creativity in your mind when you start thinking about how you can apply these actions in your own talent selection contexts and leadership. So, when you come across an example from a completely different sector or setting than the one you work or live in, don't discount it. Read on. This might be the example that will make the biggest difference for you in terms of taking innovative action in talent processes and decision-making situations.

The examples haves been designed by and written up step-by-step by Lisa and Tinna based on our years of work as leaders engaged in talent selection processes and as change makers designing inclusive talent selection processes. We also draw upon our deep experience collaborating with human resource professionals managing talent selection in organisations and with people making talent selection decisions in many organisations, projects, initiatives, and communities around the world and across a wide variety of sectors. We have collected many of the examples from other change makers. We wrote these up and sometimes added more content and behavioural insights explaining why the actions work.

The actions have been mapped to stages in the talent life cycle, along with the purpose of the actions (motivate, process, and/or frame). These offer you concrete things you can do to be inclusive. And in some cases, an action example for one phase of the talent lifecycle also might have relevancy to another phase. If you see other applications for these actions in other situations, please let us know how did you do it and how did it turn out. This is what the Inclusion Nudges global initiative is based on – sharing and reciprocity of what works.

# The Inclusion Nudges application principles

## Oh, wow!
Be prepared for innovative thinking! These will probably feel different from how you've seen inclusion approached before. This approach requires thinking and acting as a change maker and innovator.

**Be courageous!**

## Have a think!
You'll need to adapt the examples to your context. Explore what is the core of the challenge. Think about what are the stuck patterns in your work for inclusion.

**Take a deeper look!**

## Give it a go!
Use the Inclusion Nudge examples and methodology to design interventions that can work in your context. It only makes a difference if you try it out. Test it and review it!

**You can do this!**

## Share & be fair!
The authors and people sharing examples have donated their time and expertise for social change. The examples are shared to inspire, not for others to make money on.

**Join us in sharing what works!**

*To see more about the Inclusion Nudges application principles, please refer to section 6.*

Here is an overview of the 30 Inclusion Nudges in this Action Guide. These are 30 inclusive actions that you can do to make your talent selection processes and decision-making more inclusive.

## Set an Inclusive Standard

| | | |
|---|---|---|
| 1. | 'If Not, Why Not' Accountability | 71 |
| 2. | Default as 'All Jobs Are 80% Jobs' in All Job Descriptions | 75 |
| 3. | 'Flexible Work' as the Default in the Job Request Form | 79 |
| 4. | Maximum 70% Homogeneity Team Composition & Target | 83 |
| 5. | Ask Identity Data Last in a Survey or Test | 89 |

## Attract a Diverse Pool of Candidates

| | | |
|---|---|---|
| 6. | Reframe Mobility Question from Neutral to Inclusive | 94 |
| 7. | Inclusive Wording | 101 |
| 8. | Seeing Neurodiversity as an Advantage | 103 |
| 9. | Increase Women in Sales by Shifting Their Perceptions | 107 |
| 10. | Specify 'Female or Male' in Job Postings | 110 |
| 11. | Inform All About Job Openings | 113 |
| 12. | Counter Stereotypes Using Images & Social Media | 118 |

## Inclusive Evaluations & Decisions

| | | |
|---|---|---|
| 13. | Structured Scoring of 6 Qualifications | 126 |
| 14. | Anonymise People to Focus on Merit | 131 |
| 15. | Default as 'All Qualified' & 'Why Not' | 138 |
| 16. | Ask Flip Questions to Change Your Perceptions in the Moment | 143 |
| 17. | No CV Application to Reduce Biased Evaluation | 149 |
| 18. | Chunk to Debunk Bias Using Joint Evaluations | 154 |
| 19. | Colour Code People to Ensure Meritocracy | 158 |
| 20. | Neutral Observer in Evaluation Meetings | 162 |
| 21. | Put on the Gender Lens When Evaluating | 168 |
| 22. | Difference as Criterion for Selection, Not De-Selection | 172 |
| 23. | List Pros & Cons to Counter Biased Evaluations | 175 |
| 24. | Write Your Feedback Before Reading Others | 180 |

## Inclusive Interviewing

| | | |
|---|---|---|
| 25. | Interview Bundles to Bust Bias | 186 |
| 26. | The No CV Interview | 190 |
| 27. | Participate in Interview by Phone | 193 |
| 28. | Blind Interviews | 195 |
| 29. | Job Interview in Two Parts | 198 |
| 30. | Valuing Staff Contributions for Inclusive Culture | 202 |

*Now, it's time for the 30 how-to inclusive actions and your reflections.*

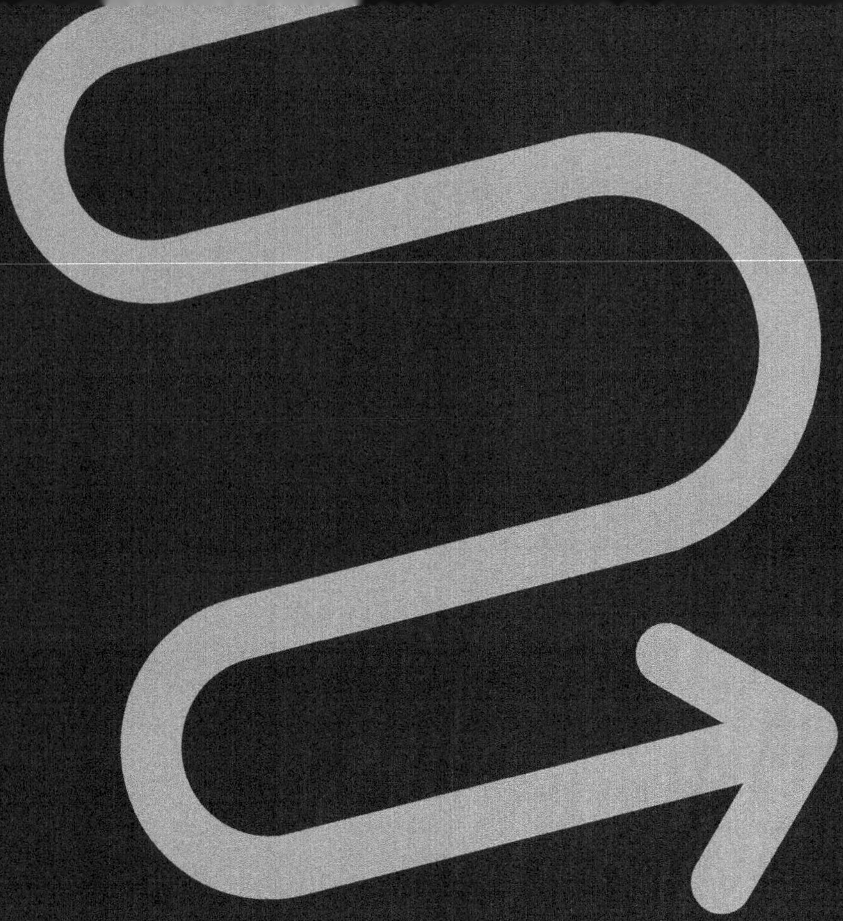

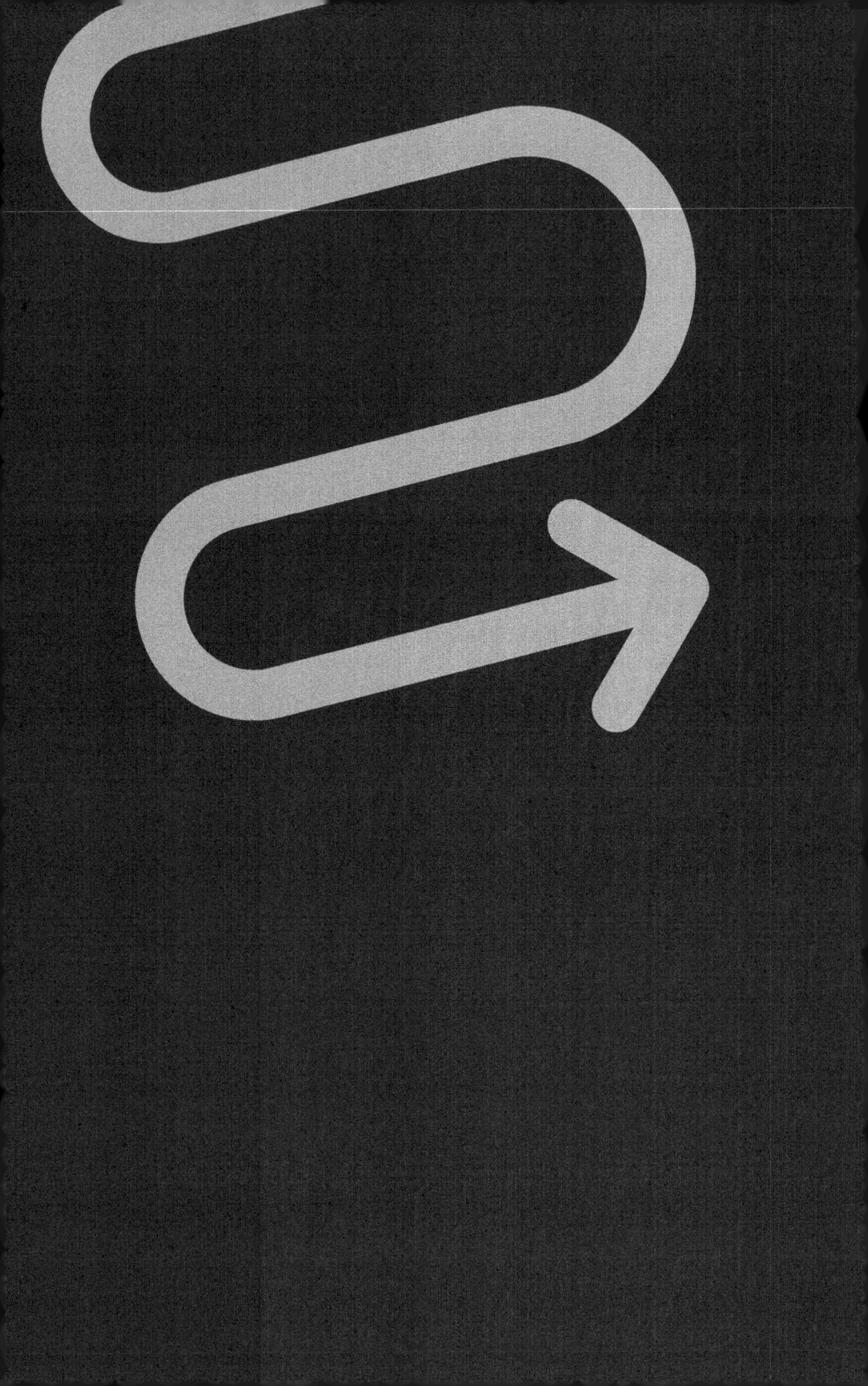

Set an Inclusive Standard

# 'If Not, Why Not' Accountability

## The Challenge

Most organisations with an inclusion, equity, & diversity program want to increase diversity among staff at all levels. Efforts include widening the talent pool, engaging with specialised search agencies, improving employer branding campaigns, establishing internal targets with senior executives reviewing for progress, leadership development training, and mentoring. Despite these actions, progress remains slow in most organisations. The intentions are good, but often actions simply reinforce the existing demographic structure. Clearly, we need an approach that involves the unconscious mind, as this is pivotal in maintaining the status quo and resisting change.

### The Inclusion Nudge

'If not, why not?' reporting to executive manager when the decision is to NOT recommend a candidate from underrepresented (minority) groups for a position or a promotion.

**Purpose:** Reporting to senior leaders makes sure hiring managers are being held accountable for their responsibility to hire and promote the best qualified and achieve more diversity and inclusion.

## How To

Make it part of the hiring and promotion process for hiring managers to report *"if not, why not"* to their executive leaders.

Most organisations have intentions and targets for increasing the diversity of their leadership. If a person from an under-represented group that is part of these targeted goals was not among those recommended for hire or promotion when a senior-level opportunity opened up, then the manager would be required (based on prior agreement from the CEO/executive leadership team) to report *"why not"* (facts) to the executive management team.

This accountability is further strengthened by requiring the selection committee to find as many facts as possible that would disaffirm or affirm the decision not to hire or promote a person from an under-represented group. Looking for facts that can explain why the candidate was not selected, as compared to the candidate that was selected, can counter biased decisions and confirmation bias.

When **Lisa Kepinski**, Founder of Inclusion Institute, was an internal inclusion and diversity leader in a multinational, there was a similar approach employed that required a 'skip level manager' discussion (so with your manager's manager) if a candidate from a minority group was not hired. A process review was conducted where the steps of the selection decision making were examined and questioned. In some cases, this occurred prior to the final decision and making an offer to the leading candidate. It resulted in some candidates getting a second look and if not given the role, they were often referred for another internal role (it was a period of rapid hiring with many open roles). In other cases, it was done post-hiring decision making. Insights from this post-review were then integrated into the hiring process, such as understanding more about the questions asked of all the candidates' during the interview and how to improve it through more behavioural-based questions.

Another way to improve judgement and decisions is to ask for facts and data that confirm or disconfirm a decision. This is crucial and should be an integrated part of all decisions because often the data sample used in decision-making processes are biased. The facts (pros and cons) should be reported to the most senior leaders as well.

This was an important learning coming out of the explosion of the NASA Space Shuttle Challenger in 1986. The investigation reveals that the engineers had presented a biased data sample of when the test flight failed but not of all the test flights including when succeeding. And no one had asked for the disconfirming data showing the opposite of the data sample. Based on this, the decision was made to launch the flight with fatal outcomes.

When making decisions based on data being presented, that data has been selected by one or more people, and in that process, they have deselected other data. You want to have access to that. Create a decision-making process where the default is that every time data is presented, it will show data for 'qualified' and 'not qualified' or pro and con or positive and negative – make sure the facts and data that shows the whole picture is the foundation for the decision.

## Authors' Comments & Behavioural Insights

A similar example focused on gender was shared in the last edition of *The Inclusion Nudges Guidebook* by **Vernā Myers**, who is now the Vice President for Inclusion Strategy at Netflix. Her example submission was based on a past discussion with a business professor who had tried it with senior leaders.

### Why it works: behavioural insights

The awareness of the procedure itself, knowing you have to report and are held accountable, is **priming** for a change of perception in the unconscious mind and for a more reflected thought process. This has more influence than the actual reporting in making a difference. When we know that others see us (see what we do and don't do), it influences our behaviour. Knowing that we will be held accountable for how we have made our decision, and what facts and data we used in our decision-making, makes us more conscious about what we base our decision on.

An interesting demonstration of the **priming effect**, was created by researcher Melissa Bateson at a university.[53] The staff paid for tea and coffee and did this by dropping money in a box on the table. A list of prices was posted on the wall above the box. For a period of ten weeks, she added a new image without explanation. Five weeks with flowers and five weeks with eyes (at the top of the price list). No one commented on this change. But the amount people paid did change. They paid almost three times as much in the 'eyes weeks' as they did in the 'flowers weeks'. This means that being watched prodded the unconscious mind to change behaviour. In this case, the effect occurred without any awareness.

In this Inclusion Nudge of 'if not, why not reporting', they are aware of being watched and that has a similar priming effect. **Priming** refers to a psychological manipulation where the presence of a stimulus (the 'prime') alters subsequent behaviour of the people experiencing the stimulus. This can be words, visuals, colours, eyes, changes in the environment, and much more. Priming has been well documented in both cognitive and social psychology, and behavioural economics. It has also been met with criticism. It might well be that the reason *'If not, why not?'* reporting works is not due to the priming effect, but due to the effects of the **social environment** faced by a decision maker. One fundamental feature of decision environments in social and organisational settings is the need for individuals to account for (or justify) their judgments to themselves and others. **Accountability** is a critical **norm enforcement mechanism**[54] that influences judgment and evaluations. This is being reinforced with 'if not, why not reporting'.

It is important to look for patterns of unintentional spin offs and negative implications, such as political correctness or hiring diversity candidates to merely meet targets or unsupported hires of diverse candidates (where they are not properly onboarded or supported in the role).

This process design is not only relevant to use when it comes to making decisions about who to hire and promote, but also when it comes to making decisions in general. For example, this can be useful when it comes to development and decisions about people, consumers, ideas, technology, markets, city planning, communities, social welfare and more. There is no limitation to where this is relevant.

**Set an Inclusive Standard**

# Default as 'All Jobs Are 80 % Jobs' in All Job Descriptions

## The Challenge

Working 80% or part-time is still seen by many organisations as the exception to the norm and as a benefit or arrangement for only certain categories of employees, notably women[55] with children (despite evidence showing that this topic is of interest to all employees across many dimensions, such as generational, geography, level, etc.).[56] As a result of part-time being associated as the exception to the norm, managers often regard it as an extra cost and burden. Furthermore, all too frequently, managers believe that a job can be carried out successfully only by a full-time employee. This may be due to blindly following traditional working models and, thus, maintaining what may be an outdated, unproductive approach. At the same time, many employees fear that asking for part-time or reduction in working hours will be career limiting. Those who choose or need to work 'differently' may be seen as lacking commitment because they do not fit the ideal norm of the always-available worker. One study found that 49% of parents don't feel comfortable talking to their employer about flexible working arrangements because of this fear of appearing uncommitted.[57] Yet, many people are not interested or able to work according to these traditional norms, and therefore may not apply to join an organisation that is not offering flexible ways of working. Also, an organisation that doesn't offer alternative ways of working risks lower employee engagement and retention.[58] These implicit norms about how to work best limit an organisation's ability to hire, retain, and promote the best qualified people.

## The Inclusion Nudge

> Change the default from all positions being full-time jobs, to all jobs being 80% positions.
> Change the argumentation burden from the employee to the manager.
>
> If the job cannot be worked 80%, the manager has to argue: 'Why not?'
> (Thus, opt out instead of opt in on this new norm of 80% jobs.)

**Purpose:** The purpose is to create a new norm where every employee has equal opportunity to work 80% or part-time as the default option. The purpose is also to change an often-dominant perception that employees who work part-time are less engaged in their work despite opposite evidence. By changing the argumentation burden, from the employees having to argue "Why I should have part-time", and this way making them argue why they have to deviate from the traditional norms of full-time, this also aims to make people working part-time feel less as outliers or as someone getting special treatment.

## How To

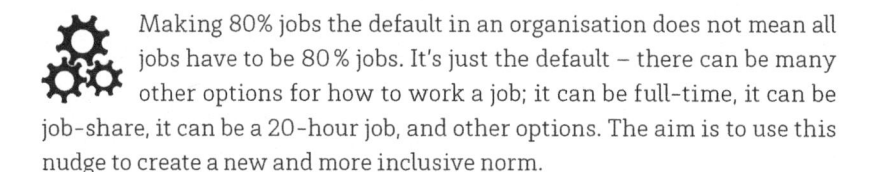

Making 80% jobs the default in an organisation does not mean all jobs have to be 80% jobs. It's just the default – there can be many other options for how to work a job; it can be full-time, it can be job-share, it can be a 20-hour job, and other options. The aim is to use this nudge to create a new and more inclusive norm.

**Tinna C. Nielsen,** Founder of Move the Elephant for Inclusiveness, and **Lisa Kepinski,** Founder of Inclusion Institute, have written this up this Inclusion Nudge based on several designs and actions that people have shared with us and from our own experiences with organisations, as well as public information on this practice. Here are the steps you can take to make it work.

→ Change all job descriptions to have the default '80 % positions'.

→ Identify where in the talent selection process, you can re-design processes, defaults, forms, and tools to make sure these support 'all jobs are 80 % positions' as the default.

→ Inform hiring managers that all jobs can be worked as an 80 % position unless proven otherwise.

→ Instruct the managers that they will have to provide the arguments and facts for why a position cannot be an 80 % position. With this shift in the argumentation default, managers will have to argue why part-time would not be possible in a particular position ('opt out' of the 'new' norm). This is instead of the employees having to argue why they should have 'special treatment' and putting the manager in a position of having to opt in on this 'special request'.

→ Post all roles as 80 % positions.

→ Align with communications internally and externally.

→ Also, communicate this in the job interview.

You can also find inspiration in the Inclusion Nudge **'FLEXIBLE WORK' AS THE DEFAULT IN THE JOB REQUEST FORM** (→ page 79).

## Impact

This Inclusion Nudge reframes perceptions of part-time work as being for only women, to being for all employees and for the whole organisation. This also helps change another dominant misperception of *'part-time jobs'* meaning these people are *'only part-time engaged'*. This is often a bias experienced by people in part-time positions (both men and women). This can potentially limit their career opportunities and limit the organisation's utility of their potential.

A new trend has emerged of The Four-Day Working Week. It was on the World Economic Forum's Annual Summit in Davos 2019. Research shows that a 4-day work week brings many positive benefits for people and organisations, such as employees feeling lower stress levels, higher levels of job satisfaction, an improved sense of work-life balance, as well as workers being 20% more productive.[59] Microsoft Japan reports that a shorter workweek has increased productivity by about 40% and overwhelmingly 92% of the employees liked it.[60] After trials, some other companies are now making this the default.

## Authors' Comments & Behavioural Insights

Everything around us is designed with a **default** (sometimes deliberately and other times by coincidence). A computer comes with a default browser instead of asking the user to choose. A traditional IT software system for recruitment comes with a default of showing the identity data of the applicants to the recruiter instead of anonymising it. The organ donation registration system in most countries is set up with a default of the person having to register instead of automatically registering them and asking them to opt out. You could say that the default design is a pre-set course of actions in a decision-making process.

The default is powerful in guiding human behaviour and choices, because the majority of people stick with the default that has been assigned. We blindly follow the default. There are several reasons for this. One is that it's effortless. Another is, that the majority believe the default is set because there is a good reason for this. Also, we tend to not change the default because deviating from the default might come at a cost and due to the **loss aversion bias** most will avoid this. Default design is proven as one of the most impactful choice architecture and nudge designs that can help people make choices in alignment with their best interest and make changes in the norms. Default design works by setting the default for the preferred choice or action instead of asking people to opt-in (effortful) and gives people the freedom to opt-out (which we rarely do). So, when the default in job descriptions is 'all jobs are full-time jobs', the norm is 'full-time job' and that will influence the evaluation of who is qualified and also the choice process. Very few hiring managers and recruiters will deviate from the norm (the default). So, it's not enough to state that your organisation supports part-time working and that's the new norm. You have to make it the default in the process, in the system, in the job descriptions.[61]

Set an Inclusive Standard

# 'Flexible Work' as the Default in the Job Request Form

## The Challenge

Often the ability to work flexibly (time, structure, location) is limited to just a few people in an organisation making flexible working an exception, even when many may wish to work in this way. For example, across all generations of the workforce, surveys show that each age group expresses a desire for more control over their ways of getting work done. For organisations, this can be a critical factor in talent attraction and retention. Done well, it can boost productivity and engagement. However, one of the common challenges is ensuring more flexible work arrangements are available for all employees, and not just positioned as for some, such as working mothers or tech workers.

> **The Inclusion Nudge**
>
> Make all roles 'flexible'
>
> Set a pre-selected default for all jobs to be 'flexible working' in the online form for job requests used by hiring managers in the organisation's recruitment process

**Purpose:** Ensure equity for all employees across all in the organisation by making flexible working the norm, rather than the exception. Setting the default to be flexible working is an effective way to make inclusion the default in the system, culture, and behaviour.

## How To

This is a simple redesign of an existing process if your organisation is already using online forms for submitting job requests. If not, this can easily be integrated in other forms or processes. You might even want to create one.

1. Automatically have as organisational-wide standard text for all job descriptions 'Flexible working is our norm'.

2. Design the online form for submitting a job request by hiring managers to have 'flexible working' as the pre-selected default for the job format.

→ You should carefully consider how you frame up alternative options for job formats other than 'flexible working', such as 'working in the office full-time'.

→ We recommend that you add a 'If not, why not' reasoning by instructing the hiring managers, if they want to opt out of the 'flexible working' job format, to document logical constraints about time and place. If they want to opt out and not support flexible working, at least that has to be a deliberate choice and not an unconscious action. The approach changes the thinking from "Can this job be done through other ways of working, such as flexibly and / or in another location?" to "Why would this job not be suitable for flexible ways of working?". That is an important difference in reasoning.

You can also use the Inclusion Nudge **'IF NOT, WHY NOT' ACCOUNTABILITY** (→ page 71) to support this change.

3. If a hiring manager choses another job format option than 'flexible working', initiate a discussion about potential solutions around 'logical constraints'

We recommend that you engage the employees in such job functions or similar jobs in co-creating solutions for a job design that makes flexible working possible to some extent. They often have important insights to do this.

4. Advertise all jobs at all levels with 'flexible working' explicitly communicated as the norm in the organisation.

Here are some other actions you can do to supplement this default design, which have been implemented in organisations that **Tinna C. Nielsen,** Founder of Move the Elephant for Inclusiveness, and **Lisa Kepinski,** Founder of Inclusion Institute, have worked with.

## A checklist

To support working in different locations (some call this 'remote work' or 'virtual working'), design a checklist with information about what kinds of support and technology people need to do some or all of their activities in a flexible manner (for example from a home office or a work hub). Don't leave this to chance. The checklist helps to ensure that managers can equally provide the same support to each employee. This reduces complexity, and thus, increases the likelihood that managers will make the changes needed for each employee to perform their best.

We recommend this checklist to be designed in a collaboration with employees, hiring manager, and human resources.

## Do an audit and show the gap

Use an evidenced-based approach by doing an audit of how many of your organisation's job descriptions actually have flexible work mentioned. In one organisation we worked with, the senior leaders believed their supportive comments for flex work would have impact, but a review of all job postings over six months showed less than 15 % actually had the words 'flexible working'. This data was shared with the senior leaders who were shocked about the gap between talking about their intentions and this actually being done as a standard practice. The 'aha' realisation from seeing the data triggered greater leadership support for the process design to make this the default in all job postings. Due to the gap between intentions and actions, it's important to design the job request submission form to have 'flexible working' as the default. This way you make it easy for managers to opt-in on flexible working because that is already the system default.

## Call it 'agile' instead of 'flexible'

**Reframe** the perceptions by using the word 'agile' instead of 'flexible'. This is a way to change the **anchor** of the thought process from a past-held perception of flexible work arrangements being a 'women's issue' to now being an organisational productivity issue with connotations to future proofing the organisation through agility. Also, reframe terms like 'virtual work' or 'remote work' (working in a location not physically with your team) to remove any negative designation of 'virtual' as not 'real' work and 'remote' as not with us or outliers. Replace these terms with 'new ways of working' or simply; 'it's just how we work here' (it's the **default**), or just call it 'work'.

## Impact

One example of an organisation using the online job request form with 'flexible working' set as the default option, is the telecommunication company Telstra headquartered in Australia. They have succeeded in making flexible working the default and norm with their 'All Roles Flex' programme. This began in 2013 with a pilot which was successful and with the CEO as the sponsor, it expanded company-wide in 2014. They saw an increase in diversity of applicants to the company and an increase in employee engagement. Their 'All Roles Flex' approach is covered on their website under the Careers section, and there are several articles written about their experience.[62]

Making 'flexible working' the norm in an organisation, increases well-being, stress reduction, retention, and engagement of staff. It can also make it easier to attract international candidates who might not be internationally mobile for relocation but are available for commuting. Additional impacts could be the potential for lower real estate needs due to less people in the office, and for society, there is less pollution from commuters every day.

## Authors' Comments & Behavioural Insights

We have seen over and over again, how organisations explicitly state that they support flexible working, but the recruitment process does not change accordingly with these intentions. It's difficult for individual managers to change the culture and norm in an organisation if the system design does not support this.

To understand the behavioural insights about the power of default design, see the Inclusion Nudge **DEFAULT AS 'ALL JOBS ARE 80% JOBS' IN ALL JOB DESCRIPTIONS** (→ page 75).

**Set an Inclusive Standard**

# Maximum 70 % Homogeneity Team Composition & Target

## The Challenge

It is often a challenge that teams are not composed in ways that ensure the right mix of diversity, people, and skills. In this way, we miss out on greater potential and innovation. Research[63] by Susanne Justesen, who is an innovation diversity advisor and the Founder of Innoversity in Copenhagen, shows that too much **homogeneity** (sameness) in a group directly impacts performance. This was measured based on the groups' ability to solve problems, make decisions, reach their deadlines, maintain their budgets, and not least of all, their overall economic performance. The direct link between performance and group homogeneity was the strongest when the homogeneity of nationality, gender, or age group (generation) did not exceed 70 % in the groups measured. That is, group performance became negatively impacted when more than 70 % of group members had the same gender, the same nationality, and/or belonged to the same age group. Research on releasing the innovative potential in teams by the London Business School found that 50:50 on gender had the biggest impact.[64]

Another challenge is the way we set targets for diversity in our organisations. We tend to focus on the minorities and gender diversity. Often, the connotations of target setting, such as 30 % women in leadership, are of a moral character with associations of *"nice to have"*. Unfortunately, this triggers unconscious perceptions that diversity is a *"women's issue"* based on bias thinking that women should be fixed and that women are hired only because they are women and not because they are competent.

To benefit from diversity in our organisations, it's important to change these stuck perceptions about diversity and to change the way we compose teams.

Diversity must have connotations to performance and innovation (this is a resource perspective) and not to minority and women. Perceptions can be reframed by setting targets based on facts about high-performing teams and diversity. Thereby, turning the diversity agenda away from being a *"nice to have"* towards rather a *"need to have"*.

Here's how **Tinna C. Nielsen** addressed this in her former role as Head of Inclusion, Diversity and Collaboration in Arla Foods.

> **The Inclusion Nudge**
>
> Set a target for the maximum similarity of various demographic factors.
>
> Set a team composition target for how to compose high-performance teams:
> A 'Maximum 70% Homogeneity' team target.
>
> → Max. 70% of team members with the same **national/ethnic background**
> → Max. 70% of team members with the same **gender**
> → Max. 70% of team members from the same **generation**
> → Max. 70% of team members from the same **educational/professional background**
>
> **Reframe the targets to be about reducing homogeneity.**

**Purpose:** Reframe perceptions as a means to achieve more diversity in teams without having to talk about diversity. Communicate diversity targets as team composition targets for better performance and to align with leaders' existing performance aspirations. By communicating your diversity targets this way, you avoid triggering perceptions that diversity is about women or minorities. Avoid communicating targets such as *"30% women"* because it fosters *"fix-the-women"* perceptions and bevaviours.

## How To

### Cluster gender with other differences
Avoid associations of women being *"the problem to fix"*. Couple gender with other differences, such as nationality and age. Also, watch for patterns of the use of *"gender"* but actually referencing only women and not the full spectrum of gender.

### Differentiate the target
Be realistic in accordance with the current pipeline and hierarchical levels. For example, the Executive Management Group and Business Group's Top Leadership teams have to reach the objective in all four factors. Other leadership teams and employee teams (including project teams) have to reach the objective in at least two factors and more if possible (if in the available recruitment base). The above example was the team objective set in Arla Foods. Add other characteristics depending on the specific reality in your situation (such as a bias towards specific universities). Set the target according to your pipeline. If you have access to more diversity, then set it as *'Maximum 50 % of the same ...'*.

### Create composition assessment tool
Use a template (a simple one-page spreadsheet) to assess the percentage of the dominant gender, nationality, generation, educational and professional background, and/or other criteria in your context. Add the number of members in the team (for example 10 people), then add how many team members out of 10 have the same nationality (don't write the nationality), how many have the same gender, how many out of 10 are from the same generation), and so on. This current team composition assessment is important to use in hiring situations to make informed decisions and increase the quality of the selection process. When you have two equally qualified candidates, look at the assessment to decide if you need a man or women to reduce the percentage of the dominant gender in order to achieve maximum 70 % homogeneity. In some cases, you might have to choose between reducing sameness in gender or generation and you will end up with a higher percentage of gender because you made a decision that generational diversity was more important for the team and the tasks at hand.

The objective does not have to be mandatory nor linked to bonuses to work. Create motivation and buy-in from leaders by showing research results and internal data that demonstrate the correlation between team composition and performance.[65] Create a **follow the herd** reaction by showcasing that the majority of 'similar others' are reaching this target, such as by communicating that *"7 out of 10 teams in your unit have achieved the target and are comprised of a mix of talents to increase innovation".*

### Design Variation

There are many ways diversity targets can contribute to alter perceptions. Here is an example of gender targets we spotted in a press release from the law firm Baker McKenzie[66] in June 2019. This 40:40:20 example illustrates how you can broaden gender goals to be more inclusive across the gender spectrum.
→ 40% women
→ 40% men
→ 20% flexible (women, men, or non-binary persons)

## Impact

The diversity-performance measures behind the 'max 70% principle' relates to teams only (when there is direct collaboration amongst the group members in question). Research shows that when the prevalence of demographic factors, such as gender, generation, and nationality, are set at a maximum of 70% on a team, then the performance is better. The profit margin is on average 3.7% higher in diverse teams versus more homogeneous teams and than in teams with a higher prevalence of the above factors.[67]

By changing targets for the representation of demographic diversity in teams and the perception about inclusion and diversity in Arla Foods, the conversation changed to be predominantly resource and performance oriented. This discourse change was driven by those who had participated in the inclusion and diversity (this was not the title) learning session (which was a bottom-up change movement). The leaders expressed their explicit support for such target setting because it resonated with performance and innovation. One leader created a tool spreadsheet to measure the composition of the current team and used this to make a fact-based and informed selection in hiring situations. The leader shared this tool with the human resource department and they shared it across the organisation.

Leaders in Arla Foods used the objective as a guiding principle in recruitment, restructuring of teams, staffing project teams, and composing work groups. And none of the leaders were being held accountable or forced to reach this goal. Instead, they worked on achieving it because it made sense for them, and that's why the reframing worked so successfully. They reported positive group dynamics and better performance in the diverse teams.

## Authors' Comments & Behavioural Insights

### Why it works: behavioural insights
### The focus matters

Setting such a target is reframing the perception of diversity as an end goal, and is instead creating a focus on reducing 'sameness' as a crucial enabler to achieving better performance and innovation. When focusing on this, you focus on the **'meaningful destination'** which is innovation and high-performance for most managers and project leaders and that **focus steers** our behaviour.

### The framing matters

With this framing you avoid triggering some of the negative feelings many people unconsciously **associate with words** such as *"diversity"* and *"gender equality"* which can be a loss of privileges, being with people who are not my in-group, feeling insecure, harder work (due to more communication), sharing power, and much more. Without mentioning *"diversity"*, this framing helps to achieve more diversity.

If a message is framed like this
*"Of one hundred patients who have this operation,
ninety are alive after five years"*
then we perceive that as a comforting message.

But if the same facts are framed like this
*"Of one hundred patients who have this operation,
ten are dead after five years"*
then we would be alarmed and perceive that as negative.

This means that it matters a lot how we present the data, including how we set targets and communicate about them. This is the case in all issues, because framing shapes our mental associations, and thus perceptions and behaviours.

The psychologists Amos Tversky and Daniel Kahneman identified the impact of framing and published their findings in the article *The Framing of Decisions and the Psychology of Choice*.[68]

**The order matters**

The order of the demographic characteristics you list in the target is important because the first information creates an **anchor** in the thought process. So, if you want to change a very common perception of *"diversity"* being about *women* and *minorities* to a perception of diversity being about all of us, make sure to list, for example, age or nationality in the beginning, instead of starting with gender (which many perceive as only *"women"*). Put gender in the middle of the demographic characteristics listing.

The pioneering research[69] on anchoring was done by Amos Tversky and Daniel Kahneman in the 1970's and is still highly relevant, especially when it comes to reframing perceptions.

Set an Inclusive Standard

# Ask Identity Data Last in a Survey or Test

## The Challenge

For over 20 years, more than 300 research studies on the impact of asking identity data prior to a test or survey have shown that this can skew the way people answer the questions and how they perform.[70] Many organisations use a variety of surveys (such as employee engagement surveys, customer/patient surveys, citizens surveys, and more) and have questions about the respondents' identity data. Also, organisations frequently conduct skills testing as part of their hiring process. Often, these ask about identity aspects, as well.

The types of questions included can cover a wide range of identity data depending on the organisation and the country, such as sex, gender (usually this is *incorrectly* limited to only two forms), age, race/ethnicity, nationality, citizenship and residency, religion, marital status, child status, household income, tenure, abilities, education level, job level, job function, past performance and grades, and more.

Without knowing, we are all influenced by questions about our identity. One way that this can show up is being asked for your identify information before taking a test or completing a survey. The identity data request activates stereotypes in the minds of the person taking the test and research has shown that it can impact performance (called **stereotype threat**). For example, if asked about gender before a math test, women and girls perform poorer than men and boys and this is even more the case if girls and women have an identity attachment to the subject (meaning it's important to them).[71] With all the efforts to increase women in STEM (science, technology, engineering, and mathematics) career fields, this can have a detrimental effect of seemingly wanting to encourage them to the field while at the same time reminding them of stereotypes that hold a view of girls and women *"don't do well at mathematics"*.

This effect has been shown in other areas as well, including how asking about ethnicity/race can impact test performance.[72] And questions about income can trigger a stereotype threat about socio-economic background and detrimental stereotypes with a negative influence on behaviour.[73] Also, asking about gender and age has also been shown to dangerously influence the quality of driving performance.[74]

> **The Inclusion Nudge**
>
> Move all identity data questions to the end of a test or survey.
>
> Do not show it in the beginning.

**Purpose:** Avoid priming and activating stereotype perceptions which may affect performance and skew responses.

## How To

Be clear on what identity data is really needed, and only ask about that.

→ Design tests and surveys to have this come only at the very end, and ideally on a separate page/webpage from the questionnaire/test.

→ Make sure to include a statement on why this data is being asked, how it will be used, and assurance of confidentiality.

## Impact

Receive better results by ensuring that the surveys and assessments are as objective as possible and not being influenced by stereotype treat.

## Authors' Comments & Behavioural Insights

We advise organisations to design their processes for applications (such as for open positions, vendor forms, grant funding, membership, etc.) to consider carefully if they need identity data and if so, what specifically is needed and then move these questions to the very end of the application.

There is more than enough evidence that these types of identity-related questions should not be asked first in surveys or tests but at the end. Yet, **Tinna C. Nielsen,** Founder of Move the Elephant for Inclusiveness, and **Lisa Kepinski,** Founder of Inclusion Institute find in their inclusion change design work with many of organisations (both in the public and private sector) that so many are still doing this without realising the potential impact on their inclusion initiatives that this framing can have.

Lisa was working with a global inter-governmental agency on their gender parity initiative. One of the steps for starting the work was completing their vendor registration form. Lisa was really shocked to see that the first questions were about her marital status and her spouse's name, age, occupation, contact details, and the names of all her children, age, and their relationship to her (biological child, step child, adopted child, etc.). These highly personal questions came *before* even asking about her business information, professional qualifications, and the statement of work that she was going to do with them. When she brought this up with the organisation, they understood the reaction, and said, *"well that vendor form was based on our application form for hiring staff"*! So, not only were they potentially activating stereotypes for their vendors, but also for applicants of internal positions with them. Needless to say, this became one of the first recommendations that Lisa made to them on their gender parity work. She did hear back that they have redesigned the form to only ask what is really need and to put those questions at the end of the form.

### Why it works: behavioural insights

**Priming** is a psychological phenomenon and is the tendency for subtle cues in our environment to influence our behaviour. These cues can be so subtle that we don't even consciously notice them. Many studies demonstrate the effects of priming across several areas.[75] Asking identity data has a priming effect. Simply having to tick a box for one's gender, age, nationality etc influences how we answer the questions in the test, survey, assessment. But even worse, it can also trigger stereotype threat, which has a negative influence proven to make people underperform. That's why moving such questions and collection of information to the end of your talent assessments and employee engagement surveys is so critical.

Setting an inclusive standard is your foundation for successful talent selection.

Priming can also have a positive impact. Research[76] shows that priming with words related to intelligence, 1 to 4 days before completing a practice exam increased performance on the midterm exam compared to neutral primes (it has a long-term effect). We suggest, that you experiment with ways to use priming when doing surveys, assessments, and tests. Make sure to test, measure, and follow up to document what works.

**WHAT & HOW**
*I'll make sure to set an inclusive standard*

**Attract a Diverse Pool of Candidates**

# Reframe Mobility Question from Neutral to Inclusive

## The Challenge

**?** In many organisations, significantly more men than women receive international assignments, which are seen as a required career experience for promotion to senior roles. This explicit requirement, assignment pattern, and implicit norms sharply narrows the pipeline of internal women for senior executive roles. There is a need to widen this pipeline to be more gender balanced (and for many organisations to be more diverse in other ways, as well).

However, some questions, which are assumed to be neutral in design, are actually generating responses that indicate the questions are not as open and fair as assumed. For example, with a question about international mobility in an organisation, where **Lisa Kepinski,** Founder of Inclusion Institute, previously worked, a majority of the women opted out of international assignments as a career option, while a majority of the men over-opted in. More men responded favourably than actually would take an international assignment if presented one. The result was that the question response pool was not valid. It was not producing the same perspective taking in men and women as they considered the question. This 'neutral' question actually was a barrier to the organisation's goals of a diverse talent pipeline for new assignments and promotions. This is what Lisa did to change the status quo.

## The Inclusion Nudge

Change a seemingly neutral question about international mobility to an inclusive question.

The question in the talent process was changed from:
"Are you internationally mobile?"

To this question:
"Would you consider an international assignment at some point in the future?"

**Purpose:** Reframe and redesign the question to shift perceptions to be more inclusive of diverse orientations of all people and to build a wider talent pipeline for future opportunities. This framing changes the anchor of the thought process, and thus changes the answer to the question.

## How To

In the organisation where this framing action was designed, when filling in personal profiles in the talent management system, significantly more men than women answered *"yes"* to the question *"Are you internationally mobile?"*

This was a problem because answering *"no"* would have negative implications for career options and was a loss of good talents to enable the success of the organisation in other countries. Here's how this challenge was addressed.

### ❶ Analysis
Conduct extensive organisational research to reveal patterns of potential gender bias in the employee life cycle and organisational culture. Look for what human resource data reveals – where do the numbers change?

Results from this example's organisational assessment showed the gender gap in who had international assignments. A deeper look showed that the first-choice moment for an international assignment rested with the employee's answer to one question in their online talent profile. The question was *"Are you internationally mobile?"*

Lisa conducted interviews and focus groups to understand from which perspectives the question was being answered by people. And also, to explore if there is a mismatch with what the numbers show and actual aspirations.

She found that women tended to answer *"no"* due to reflection about the current moment, especially thoughts of home and life demands *("How will I ever get everything arranged? So much is depending on me to be here and available.")*. They answered from a **present orientation.** Men, however, tended to answer *"yes"* *("I'll sort it out when the time comes. There's no firm offer right now.")*. They answered from a **future orientation.** She also found that the number of women answering *"yes"* did not match the much larger number of women who said in the audit discussions that they actually would like to have an international career.

A further challenge was that the phrase of *'internationally mobile'* often was perceived by the women as a total relocation (as an all-or-nothing situation), which meant broader consequences for the employees and their family. However, the reality of the international assignment offer was that of a temporary situation with variable time frames and different living situations. So, the question itself was not aligned with the true intended outcome of building a talent pipeline for international work which entailed many different forms.

## ❷ Design

The design goal was to align with your intention of being inclusive of all. Lisa's organisation did this by changing the question with the purpose of framing it to be as neutral as possible and to instead get people to answer from the same orientation (present/future). The *Framing Perception* Inclusion Nudge put in place in this organisation was to change the question to be,

*"Would you consider an international assignment at some point in the future?"*

**③ Verify**

Test the question on a wide range of diverse staff before implementing. Test various ways of framing the question to make sure you implement the most inclusive framing.

## Impact

By simply reframing one question, more women (more than a 25% increase in one year) said they would consider an international assignment. It's not that 25% more women were all of a sudden internationally mobile, but that 25% more women answered yes, due to a change in perception of the implications of answering yes. It can be assumed that in this case women answered the original question from a present frame of reference, thinking about the consequences on their private lives, and thus, being more reluctant. Whereas, men would answer from a future frame of reference, thinking this could work out when there is an actual offer later on. And it can also be assumed that men would answer *"yes"* based on insights that being registered as internationally mobile would further their career opportunities (which is in alignment with men applying to jobs when they master about 60% of the required skills and women when mastering 100%).

Lisa shares that one of the biggest obstacles to overcome in making this change was from the IT department that said the number of characters in the new question were too many for the space in the online talent management system. It wasn't that the IT colleagues didn't get the need for the change to happen or that they didn't have the skills to do it. It was that they didn't feel empowered to incur the expense to make the change to the online talent platform.

This involved another level of analysis to accomplish the change from this Inclusion Nudge. Lisa flipped her own perception of seeing resistance *("IT won't do this!")* to one of collaboration *("Who is the client of IT that can request this change to happen and enable IT to become a change partner in this redesign?")*. That perspective helped to identify who else needed to be engaged in the change process and to authorise the needed IT redesign work to complete this Inclusion Nudge implementation.

## Authors' Comments & Behavioural Insights

This Inclusion Nudge was designed by Lisa when she worked as an internal inclusion and diversity leader in a multinational corporation, but reframing a seemingly neutral question like this, is applicable in all organisations because they will all be fighting for skilled talent in a global workforce. One critical trend in the labour market is an increased demand for highly skilled workers and a shortage in the future. This means that also organisations with a domestic orientation will need to make themselves attractive to skilled talent across borders. Questions like *"Would you be agile to work on international assignments for short periods of time?"* or *"Would you consider commuting to work in various locations?"* could be relevant. We recommend that you experiment with the powerful technique of reframing seemingly neutral questions to be inclusive in as many organisational areas as possible.

With this Inclusion Nudge example, the challenge is to better achieve a wide pool of employees who are actually open to international assignments. Many organisations can get stuck if they take an approach of blaming the women (or other diverse people that they are seeking to increase). This is usually automatically driven by stereotypes and established norms. It can be easier to think that the problem lies with the person, rather than with the organisation's own systems, cultural patterns, and decisions. Consider comments such as these below.

*"Well, these women just don't want to leave their current homes."*
*"These women are not ambitious enough for such stretch assignments."*
*"These women lack the confidence for international leadership."*

When these are expressed, then the opportunity to change the pattern is misdirected and lost is the leveraging of a wider source of talent.

However, for organisations that want to de-bias their systems, the starting point is with the actual decision moment. This is called **choice architecture** in behavioural economics terms. For this case of the international assignment talent pool, the de-biasing design process was to look at the actual question itself. Why were more men responding positively to the question, and why were more women responding negatively to the question? Deeper analysis revealed that men and women did not perceive the question in the same way. Research also shows that words appeal differently to men and women, and to people with other types of differences (such as nationality, age group, and others).

This Inclusion Nudge was one of the first examples that Lisa shared with Tinna when they met in 2013. When Tinna, with excitement, suggested (based on the evidence) a reframing of the question about international mobility in the multinational where she worked at that time, she was met with a high level of scepticism from her human resource colleagues. They rejected the suggestion with the argument that the main problem was not so much the women who did not answer *'yes'*. The main problem was according to them, that many men answered *'yes'*, but would actually not be internationally mobile when the offer of international assignments were suggested to them. So, in this context, implementing this Inclusion Nudge might not be enough to make sure the reframing would fit the problem. It would require an assessment to explore the root cause of the issue in this specific organisational case and to design and test several questions to find the questions that would fit the problem.

We share this experience here to make a point that one intervention rarely fits all contexts. Use the examples of Inclusion Nudges to get inspiration and make sure to customise these to fit the context and specific issues in your organisation.

So, how did it turn out in the organisation where Tinna worked? Well, the question was not changed centrally by HR, but Tinna shared the example with many leaders in the organisation. As they understood the behavioural insights behind the design, the leaders started identifying questions they should consider to reframe. They started talking about 'international mobility' differently to focus more on 'international assignments' (this also matched a realisation in the organisation that a total relocation of employees was not effective enough and it was difficult to ensure cultural integration of the family). The reframing fit the organisational context.

### Why it works: behavioural insights
Having the same frame of reference to get the most accurate responses to questions is critical to produce accurate results. In this example, the **anchoring of perspective** of the time frame of *present* versus *future* was a variable in people's experience of the question. The way the original question was composed, it simply did not provide enough context

to frame to the same view of what was being asked. An inclusive reference point is important in question design. Because we can all fall prey to biases influencing our question designs, we should seek out ways to hear others' views on the question before its implemented.

This is often described in nudge theory as the **"power of the small"**. The actual example in this case is seemingly of a small and simple change of rewording one question. But the level of research and analysis behind it, the time and engagement of others, and the measuring and testing were all actually quite intensive work. But the power of this small change (nudge) can have a big impact on the employees' career opportunities and organisation's success.

Attract a Diverse Pool of Candidates

# Inclusive Wording

## The Challenge

The language used in job postings can be a limiting factor in who applies. For example, a recent research report showed that *"if the word 'aggressive' was included in a job description, 44% of women and 33% of men would be discouraged from applying for the role."*[77] Yet, more than 50,000 job postings on LinkedIn contain *'aggressive'*.[78]

### The Inclusion Nudge

Use an inclusive language checker for job descriptions as an integrated part of your talent attraction process.

**Purpose:** Ensure the language in job descriptions is equally attracting all potential talents and not excluding them.

## How To

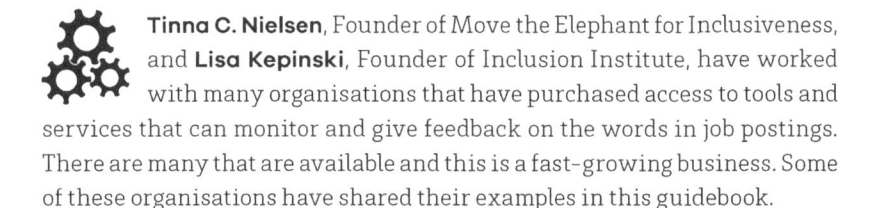

**Tinna C. Nielsen**, Founder of Move the Elephant for Inclusiveness, and **Lisa Kepinski**, Founder of Inclusion Institute, have worked with many organisations that have purchased access to tools and services that can monitor and give feedback on the words in job postings. There are many that are available and this is a fast-growing business. Some of these organisations have shared their examples in this guidebook.

Here is one with a unique twist that has recently been announced called the Spellcheck for Bias from the **Geena Davis Institute on Gender in Media** and the **University of Southern California Viterbi School of Engineering**. Together, they developed this tool.[79] Disney is the first to use this with their film and TV scripts. The tool analyses the scripts by tracking gender and other biases by examining aspects such as the number of male and female characters, LGBTQIA community characters, race/ethnicity of characters, characters with disabilities, etc.[80] The advantage of this tool is that it occurs prior to production, and thus it is easier to make changes when presented with the analysis which shows how biases inadvertently cropped up in script writing. It is also good that this tool pushes beyond the traditional gender-only focus of some other tools.

However, it's important to note that not all organisations have their needs fully met by tools that are available on the market or they may not have the budget that such tools can require. We've also worked with groups that have created their own internal monitoring tool based on the unique language in their sector or for certain types of roles. But this too can require resources to develop such a tool. So, to get going, we're really pleased to share about this great free tool to check the language in your job postings (see below).

## Publicly Available Resources

**The Gender Decoder for Job Adverts** by **Kat Matfield**. Kat's tool has been used by many who, like us, really appreciate this contribution to help remove bias from job postings and to make this free access to all. See: http://gender-decoder.katmatfield.com/

We understand that Kat is from a technology background and felt compelled to do something to help mitigate bias in the sector. Kat self-developed this tool and released it free for all to use. We, and many others, have appreciated Kat's contribution to de-bias and nudge for good.

Try it out by reviewing the language used in multiple processes such as performance evaluations, recognitions of accomplishments, case studies, talent attraction communication. Look for patterns, stereotypes, and biases in how women and men, age groups, abilities, nationalities, ethnicities, and others are described. The language used does matter in terms of who applies and how diverse are the pool of candidates.

Attract a Diverse Pool of Candidates

# Seeing Neurodiversity as an Advantage

## The Challenge

People on the autism spectrum often face stigma, discrimination, human rights violations, and limited career opportunities – with some reporting unemployment at 80 %.[81] Many studies have pointed out that people with autism often have excellent skills in memory, focus on details, innovation and creativity, and pattern-spotting.[82]

There are many dedicated organisations who are working to ensure that equal employment opportunities are inclusive of people on the autism spectrum and of people with other neurological abilities. Unexamined biases can interfere with our best intentions to have an inclusive workplace with equal opportunities for people with a wide range of neurodiversity. The terms we use is a challenge because these reinforce associations about people with autism as a "burden" and "challenge". We need to reframe this to be a "resource", so organisations see their abilities as an asset. The **United Nations** and **Specialisterne** do it this way.

### The Inclusion Nudge

To help support commitments to hire people with diverse neurological abilities, replace the term 'autistic people' with **"Autism Advantage"** and **"Neurodiverse Talent"**

**Purpose:** Counter the unconscious stereotypes and assumptions about people who are different from the majority neurological style, sometimes called *"neuro-typical"*.

## How To

For this kind of challenge, it's rarely enough to reframe perceptions, the processes in an organisation have to be designed to support the hiring and integration of all talent, including neurodiverse talent.

→ Screen and revise all job descriptions and role requirements to ensure these do not rule out neurodiverse talent by having requirements such as 'being a team player, emotional intelligence, persuasiveness.'[83]

→ Invite neurodiverse talents to help you co-create a tool to identify excluding wording and ensure inclusive wording in job descriptions and job adverts.

See the Inclusion Nudge **INCLUSIVE WORDING** (→ page 101) for inspiration and to combine with screening for gender-bias and other stereotypes.

→ Use work-specific tests where candidates solve some of the typical tasks in the job. Let them show their skills instead of using traditional interviews.

Use the Inclusion Nudges **STRUCTURED SCORING OF 6 QUALIFICATIONS** (→ page 126) for inspiration of work-related tests and for de-biasing the rating and selection of talent.

→ Review your (internal and external) communication for how the value of diversity is expressed. Make sure to include descriptions and real life examples of how neuro-diversity is a resource (for your organisation, community, city, customers, products, people, etc.).,

You can also create a supporting *Feel the Need* Inclusion Nudge to get people onboard with your initiative to employ neurodiverse talents. Do this by sharing information from research on the advantages of having employees who are neurodiverse. Do it in a way that emphasises the loss if these talented people are not in your workforce (trigger the **loss aversion** bias). In the *Action Guide for Motivating Allies*, you can find inspiration how to do this in the 30 examples of *Feel the Need* Inclusion Nudges and *Framing Perceptions* Inclusion Nudges.

## Authors' Comments & Behavioural Insights

### Why it works: behavioural insights

We use two dominate criteria to assess others—warmth and competency. Studies by Cuddy, Fiske, & Glick that look at our judgements of others by **social groups**, reveal patterns of unconscious bias and stereotypes. For example, when thinking about people with 'disabilities' as a group, their research shows a judgement pattern of ratings high on warmth, but low on competency. This pattern has **impact on our emotions** (pity) and behaviour such as active helping and passive neglect, thus limited engagement. But our perception of others and our behaviour are also dependent of context. Research shows that in a work context persons with disability are systematically associated with less warmth than persons without disability and with less competence.[84] This also reinforces to an unconscious norm of what is perceived as 'able-bodied' (the implicit mental association of people without disabilities).

The results can be exclusion and limited opportunities for people with different abilities (which may include ourselves at some point in our lives) and a loss of valuable talent for organisations.

Reframing 'autistic people' to 'neurodiverse talent' helps to flip the perspective from a negative, damaging stereotype. It also re-sets the default in our minds, cultures, and organisational processes from 'neuro-typical' (the existing dominant style of neurological abilities) to one that is more inclusive of a wider range of neurological abilities.

By having more personal interaction with people who are different to ourselves, we can raise our comfort level with 'difference', develop new mental models that interrupt automatic stereotypes[85], and we can reframe *'disabilities'* into *'abilities'*.

Keep in mind, everyone is searching for the best talent. Finding the best qualified person that can bring value to your team, organisation, and community is all about how diverse is the pool of candidates that you attract. You never know who is the best and you want to make sure you don't miss out by narrowing who you attract. We hope this gives you inspiration to think broader and take action for more diversity and inclusion.

## Publicly Available Resources

Learn more about the **Specialisterne Foundation** and 'The Specialist' Concept for employing people with autism. by visiting their website at
http://specialisterne.com/

The **United Nations** has declared the 2nd of April as World Autism Awareness Day. You can learn more about this at the UN's web page found at https://www.un.org/en/events/autismday/

Attract a Diverse Pool of Candidates

# Increase Women in Sales by Shifting Their Perception

## The Challenge

There were less women than men in business customer-facing sales roles in this tech company. There was an intent to achieve a gender balance in the sales function, and the incoming graduates' intern program was one of the focal points to begin working on this goal. Despite senior leadership, human resources, hiring managers, and the sales function all coming together to support this goal, women were not expressing interest in a sales internship, despite them having the qualifications. **Lut Nelissen**, then the General Western Europe HR Director, and **Lisa Kepinski,** who was then the EMEA Diversity & Inclusion Director at Hewlett-Packard, share how they addressed this challenge.

### The Inclusion Nudge

Reframe the sales role description to include needed skills: "collaboration, understanding the customer, providing helpful service, seeking a win-win solution" to counter stereotypical perceptions of sales as "highly masculine, competitive, aggressive".

Profile successful women and men in sales roles in recruiting material where they describe why they like their profession and what it is really like.

**Purpose:** Steer women to envision themselves in a sales role or even as a longer-term career focus, and more accurately represent the actual skills needed for a sales role in the organisation.

## How To

Carefully study and inquire into how women university graduates perceive the sales role. In this company, the assessment revealed dominant perceptions of sales as *"highly masculine, competitive, aggressive"* which were rather like the outdated 1950's style of business. However, in reality, this was no longer the overall nature of sales in this company. Instead it was about *"collaboration, understanding the customer, providing helpful service, seeking a win-win solution."*

→ To help shift the perception of the women university graduates, the position description was rewritten to include many of the above descriptions to more accurately reflect the role.

→ Also, several successful women and men in sales roles were profiled in recruiting material where they described in their own words why they liked their profession, what it was really like, and highlighted the above descriptions.

→ And many of these sales leaders were on hand at job recruiting fairs in universities to be able to immediately respond to any misperceptions of what a sales role is like.

## Impact

Changing the framing from what the sales role was being perceived as, to instead more accurately reflect the reality, resulted in more women university graduates signing up to participate in the sales internship program. Male graduates still signed up (no reductions due to the re-framing). The company had a wider talent pool. All were better informed about the true picture of the role. It also helped to reinforce the organisation's culture norms for how salespeople should behave and will be assessed.

## Authors' Comments & Behavioural Insights

It can be hard to spot the influence of implicit associations and activated stereotypes. So, it's a valuable opportunity when we are alerted that this is happening. Realising the mismatch between the job description and how female university graduates perceived what is a sales role, resulted in changing the wording, content, and style of the job descriptions to better match this. These changes had an internal impact on both women, men, and the organisation.

This kind of change has also shown to lead to redesigning for inclusion in other areas. One example is in designing accessible solutions for people with limited abilities also makes the products more appealing to a much wider customer base through new designs for simplicity and ease of use. Another example is seen with flexible work programs which often have been originally targeted to working mothers but have become a more innovative, productive, and sustainable way for all to work in the organisation. Designing for all can have impact for all, and the framing needs to reflect this.

**Attract a Diverse Pool of Candidates**

# Specify 'Female or Male' in Job Postings

## The Challenge

In the Swarovski corporation where this Inclusion Nudge was designed by **Alberto Platz**, when he was the Vice President for Global Talent & Engagement, they had a challenge to increase the number of female candidates responding to a job offer or when applying for a position. In many cases only male candidates applied. It turns out that women weren't attracted because the wording of job offers sounded unconsciously masculine.

### The Inclusion Nudge

Specify "female or male" in the titles of all job postings.

"Female or Male Head of Business Support"

Add in the text
"We are looking for a female or male motivated talent."

**Purpose:** Appeal to and attract qualified candidates of all genders, and open the thinking of the hiring manager to ensure that both men and women have equal opportunities to be considered for the role.

## How To

Revise all job postings to include both genders in the titles and descriptions.

Here is an example spotted by **Tinna C. Nielsen** in *The Economist*. This example illustrates how you can broaden gender categories to be more inclusive: **(f/m/x) is in the title.**

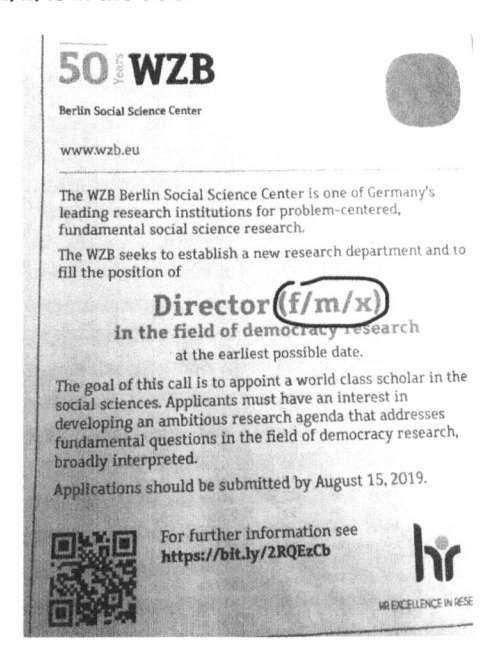

> **50 Years WZB**
> Berlin Social Science Center
> www.wzb.eu
>
> The WZB Berlin Social Science Center is one of Germany's leading research institutions for problem-centered, fundamental social science research.
>
> The WZB seeks to establish a new research department and to fill the position of
>
> **Director (f/m/x)**
> in the field of democracy research
> at the earliest possible date.
>
> The goal of this call is to appoint a world class scholar in the social sciences. Applicants must have an interest in developing an ambitious research agenda that addresses fundamental questions in the field of democracy research, broadly interpreted.
>
> Applications should be submitted by August 15, 2019.
>
> For further information see
> https://bit.ly/2RQEzCb
>
> HR EXCELLENCE IN RESE

*Photo taken by Tinna C. Nielsen of a job posting in The Economist, July 2019*

By adding 'X', the company includes all people regardless of their gender identity. This kind of broad definition can be done for other categories that require balance, including age, race, disabilities, religion, sexual orientation, and nationality.

## Impact

Alberto shared that this intervention opened up the minds of managers to focus on both women and men as applicants.

## Authors' Comments & Behavioural Insights

This is such a simple way to appeal to a diverse pool of people and make them feel welcome by simply highlighting diversity with letters F/M/X. When writing a job posting, it is a fine balance to be inclusive by highlighting diversity without excluding.

We also recommend that you always test your job postings internally with a diverse group of employees and get their input on how they perceive the wording. This is an powerful way of an creating an inclusive organisation, but unfortunately, this is a process step that is often skipped in internal development work.

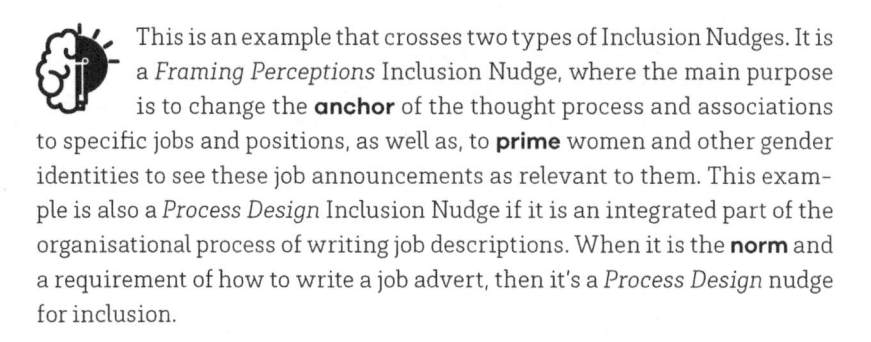

This is an example that crosses two types of Inclusion Nudges. It is a *Framing Perceptions* Inclusion Nudge, where the main purpose is to change the **anchor** of the thought process and associations to specific jobs and positions, as well as, to **prime** women and other gender identities to see these job announcements as relevant to them. This example is also a *Process Design* Inclusion Nudge if it is an integrated part of the organisational process of writing job descriptions. When it is the **norm** and a requirement of how to write a job advert, then it's a *Process Design* nudge for inclusion.

Attract a Diverse Pool of Candidates

# Inform All About Job Openings

## The Challenge

Organisations often express an intention of wanting to have more diversity in their leadership to enhance agility, decision making, and innovation. To achieve this, sometimes interventions need to be designed for early in the process, such as at the job posting and application stages.

**Sarah Kaiser**, the Global Head of Diversity and Inclusion at Fidelity International shared this example from one of her former organisations. In this case, there was a business transformation with 11 internally advertised open leadership roles for a new services model. They found that they did not get a gender diverse applicant pool (only 2 women applied out of 54 applications received). They were conscious of the research showing that women are more likely to rule themselves out if they aren't a completely perfect fit with all the job criteria. Taking this on-board, they looked at their process and practices within the organisation to see how to shift this pattern of too few women applying for leadership openings.

**Lisa Kepinski**, Founder of Inclusion Institute, saw in an organisation where she worked, a pattern of employees from various diverse backgrounds not applying for openings, especially promotional ones. She conducted interviews with many, and found that some employees were holding back on looking for new roles and applying for them. They felt they were at a disadvantage by their difference to the majority profile and felt a lack of encouraging support. Hiring managers were frustrated, stating that they would like to have difference in the applicant pool, and saw that as a positive for selection. Managers were also frustrated as the organisational culture held a talent development approach of the employees were expected to drive their own careers. Taking this on-board, they redesigned the job announcement process by changing the communication steps.

> **The Inclusion Nudge**
>
> Use targeted, personalised e-mails as a communication default for internal job openings to encourage all talents to consider applying.
>
> Also, ask the women or talents from underrepresented groups who decide not to apply to share the reasons 'Why not'.

**Purpose:** Change the job announcement communication default to ensure that all talents know about open roles and feel supported to apply. Shift thinking from an internal self-belief of *"I'm not qualified"* to *"I am seen as a strong candidate and should apply"* by using personal communications from senior leaders and influencers.

## How To

There are two versions of this *Process Design* Inclusion Nudge. These are described below.

### Version 1: Leverage role models

In one organisation, Sarah shares that they designed a personal message and invitation. The Head of Transformation, who is a woman, is seen as a role model, and sits on the board of this organisation, made it an integrated part of the recruitment process to send a personal email to all women working in customer-facing roles at senior levels in the organisation. The message was highly personal and was addressed to the recipient as

*"Senior women currently making a difference all across our organisation"*

In this message, she set out how important it was to the leadership team to address the gender imbalance in senior leadership roles. She explained the gender research and asked the women to consider why they are suitable for the roles, rather than why they are not. Women were told that if they registered interest in one of the roles, then the deadline could be extended to allow them to complete the application process. It was always a person sending the message out to ensure that it would feel personal instead of sending it from the system.

Sarah further shares that she designed an approach of also getting feedback. To improve the recruiting process she asked the women who decided not to apply to tell them the reasons why not.

### Version 2: Leverage employee groups

In Lisa's organisation, they implemented an automated process targeting when new roles were opened in the staffing system (set at a certain seniority level, such as manager level and senior project manager/technical-lead level). In addition to the normal posting on the internal online jobs site, there was an email automatically sent to members of the organisation's Employee Resource Groups (ERGs). The email steered attention to look at this role and also encouraged that they share about the opening with others in their network.

## Impact

Sarah reports that their email was sent to 80 women. It generated 6 new applications to the leadership roles and 23 pieces of feedback and reasons from the women about why they did not apply. From the feedback, new insights were gained into a number of steps that could be taken to make the leadership culture more appealing to and more supportive of women. All of these steps were endorsed by the leadership team.

Sarah showed the feedback statements to the senior leaders to 'hold up a mirror' (this is a *Feel the Need* Inclusion Nudges) and help them see a reality that was invisible to them. This was important since the senior leaders were part of a culture driven by logical data-driven discussions. They did not talk about feelings. As they read these statements from the women about their experience with and perception of a masculine company culture and the implications, they talked about feelings. As a result of this, they made a role for Sarah to participate in the meetings and hold up a mirror for the leaders to better understand the cultural patterns and where they needed to redesign the existing recruiting process to more inclusive for all.

Lisa's organisation had a major increase in the number of diverse (different from the majority) employees applying for roles. This one automated email process design resulted in a very effective way to widen the applicant pools, not only through internal employees but many shared with members of their community groups outside of work. Employee Resource Group members also talked about the impact of receiving the email as feeling that they were invited and welcomed to apply. This shifted perception from a 'closed door' to an 'open door'.

## Authors' Comments & Behavioural Insights:

### Why it works: behavioural insights
For these two *Process Design* Inclusion Nudges, several behavioural insights have been applied. These are described below.

### Shift the default & change the status quo
This personal appeal is helpful to shift the thinking by some people from the **default.** In this case, it was *"I am not qualified"*, or *"I am not seen as qualified"*, or *"I would not be selected"*. These types of default internal messages occur unconsciously. However, this unreflective default thinking may actually not accurately reflect what we wish and without addressing it, this type of shortcut thinking can influence our decisions and behaviour. In this example, it led to women not applying for the open leadership roles. Actions are needed to shift away from the default thinking and **change the status quo**. The solution needs to tap into the powerful aspects of behavioural science design, and this personalised email approach as part of the recruiting process does that. It creates another option of thinking and potential action.

### The 'personal' is powerful!
This Inclusion Nudge leverages human relationships to trigger behavioural change. A study conducted by the UK Behavioural Insights Team (BIT) focused on increasing charitable giving by employees in the workplace found that when a personalised email from the CEO to employees was sent out, the employee donations increased. This was much more effective than a generic email. And donations even more increased when an email was sent out by a colleague who had already donated and it had a picture of the people who have already donated. This draws upon the "**the peer effect,** *by making acts of giving more visibility to others within one's social group ... [and by] es-*

*tablishing **group norms** around which subsequent donors **anchor** their own gifts"*[86] (impacting the decisions and actions). In Sarah's case, the fact that the personal email was sent to women from a woman (a peer and admired role model) can have an impact, and in Lisa's case, the fact that employees sent it to other colleagues and also to their network, can have an impact.

**Show what people say ... it matters**
Sarah's example does a good step of gathering insights on why women did not apply. To see what could be done with that type of insight, look at the *Feel the Need* Inclusion Nudges in *The Inclusion Nudges Guidebook,* or in the *Action Guide for Motivating Allies.*

Attract a Diverse Pool of Candidates

# Counter Stereotypes Using Images & Social Media

## The Challenge

One of the most prevalent mental shortcuts occurring in our unconscious thinking is the categorisation of people against a set of expectations of what we think *'people like this should be'*. This comparison happens with how we perceive what is the *'appropriate'* behaviour, language, styles, appearances, hobbies, professions, and so many other areas for people based on their gender, race, ethnicity, nationality, age, abilities, sexual orientation, role in an organisation, etc. We make these snap judgements about others measured against stereotypes without even realising it.

**Isis Anchalee**[87] encountered this in 2015. She was a full-stack engineer at the San Francisco-based organisation called OneLogin.

She was asked to take part in the company's recruiting campaign where real employees' photos were used (rather than from photo stock). Here is the advertisement that featured Isis.

*Images from "You May Have Seen My Face On BART",
Isis Anchalee, Medium, 2 August 2015*

As she shares in her published article,[88] she was not prepared for the level of attention that this generated, ranging from positive to shocking. In her article, Isis says that, *"The reality is that most people are well intentioned but genuinely blind to a lot of the crap that those who do not identify as male have to deal with."* She further adds that many of the men who made negative comments were *"not bad people"* and were exemplifying the problems in the technology sector of a lack of understanding, empathy, and responsibility for inclusion and respect across diversity. Isis writes, *"This industry's culture fosters an unconscious lack of sensitivity towards those who do not fit a certain mold. I'm sure that every other woman and non-male identifying person in this field has a long list of mild to extreme personal offenses that they've just had to tolerate. I'm not trying to get anyone in trouble, fired or ruin anyone's life. I just want to make it clear that we are all humans, and there are certain patterns of behaviour that no one should have to tolerate while in a professional environment."*

This led Isis to start a campaign of **"This Is What an Engineer Looks Like ..."** and created the hashtag **#ILookLikeAnEngineer**. This campaign's goal was to re-frame perceptions that counter stereotypes of engineers by showing the wide range of people who are in fact real engineers. Isis says that *"#ILookLikeAnEngineer is intentionally not gender-specific. External appearances and the number of X chromosomes a person has is hardly a measure of engineering ability. My goal is to help redefine 'what an engineer should look like' because I think that is a step towards eliminating subconscious bias towards diversity in tech."*[89]

## The Inclusion Nudge

Post photos and messages that counter stereotypes about 'how an engineer looks'

This is Isis' first posting.

*Image from "You May Have Seen My Face On BART", Isis Anchalee, Medium, 2 August 2015*

**Purpose:** Show what engineers look like by offering visual alternatives to stereotypes. Inspire others to consider working in engineering (or other professions) even if they don't reflect the preconceptions (stereotypes) and/or the current majority population.

## How To

Using the power of social media, create a hashtag, explain your campaign, and post. This was launched by one person, and it went viral. It began based on Isis' personal experience of stereotyping and negative reactions to her not fitting some people's expectations of what an engineer 'should be'. It grew by hitting upon experiences that many others had as well.

Shortly after launching, **Michelle Glauser** and a team of people from **LadyNerds** joined in to help crowdfund to raise money for ads and billboards. The purpose of the ads was to do the following.

- → Give visibility to and normalise non-stereotypical engineers.
- → Increase awareness of discrimination that non-stereotypical engineers are facing.
- → Encourage an atmosphere of inclusion in tech.
- → Inspire people who may not have thought of being engineers before to learn engineering skills.[90]

Here is one of the ads that appeared in the San Francisco area.

*Image from #ILOOKLIKEANENGINEER Ads Start Going Up in The Bay Area This Week! Michelle Glauser, Medium 14 September 2015*

Within 10 days, as Michelle Glauser writes, there was a public event *"to gather people in the San Francisco Bay Area who had connected with the campaign in some way and to raise money for the #ILookLikeAnEngineer billboard we hoped to put up to raise awareness and inspiration, and normalize non-stereotypical engineers."*[91] The event was sold out.

## Impact

This *"started with a recruitment campaign gone wrong, but #ILookLikeAnEngineer has now become one of the most powerful hashtags ... and it's totally changed the conversation about stereotypes in the field."*[92] In just one year, more than 25,000 people shared their tweets, images, and stories by leveraging a relevant form of communication to the tech sector.[93] Isis said that *"Never in a million years would I have guessed that one year later people would still be proudly sharing the hashtag and using it as a source for building community."* Examples have been from both women and men of all different identities and backgrounds, and in a wide range of settings from the Space Station, the White House, science labs, entertainment, and many others.[94] This shows the power that one person's seemingly simple act can spark. Isis said, *"I wrote a blog post that went viral and accidentally started a global movement."*[95]

## Authors' Comments & Behavioural Insights

### Why it works: behavioural insights

Recent reviews of images in the media and digital media platforms revealed the persistence of masculine-identity as the perception prototype ('the norm') of people who work in the tech sector.[96] This has implications that women and under-represented minorities in tech are perceived as the outliers, and when compared to the male prototype "women must be exceptional, and women of color must be better than exceptional."[97] By offering **counter-culture images** on a wide scale and over a period of time, we help to shift the perceptions of the prototype. This weakens the **stereotype** (biased association).

A body of research has documented how stereotypes of women (such as being poor at math or not good in technical domains) negatively affect the performance and retention of women in STEM fields. When looking closer at how these stereotypes are manifested and maintained, it turns out that there is a profound effect of **images** on self-perception, aspirations, and performance. We should pay much more attention to this. The solutions for how to change this are often simpler and more tangible than expected.

The #ILookLikeAnEngineer campaign works because it shows a more nuanced reality than the stereotypes, but it also does more than that. It portrays **roles models** and that has a significant impact both on performance and on changing stereotypes. One study shows that exposing women to information about women in counter-stereotypical leadership positions (such as famous female judges, business leaders, scientists, politicians, and more), made them more likely to automatically associate women with leadership qualities (than the control group that had been exposed to information about flowers). Exposure to female role models not only reduced stereotypical beliefs, but it also **activated more counter-stereotypical beliefs,** such as positive beliefs about women as leaders.[98] Another study documents, that seeing pictures of successful women before having to perform can actually improve the performance of women because it circumvents the **stereotype threat** (for instance that of 'women not being good at xx').[99]

**Images** have a much bigger effect than we tend to believe. One study focused on how the gender difference in interest in computer science was influenced by exposure to stereotypical **environments** associated with computer scientists. This study showed that changing the objects in a computer science classroom from those considered stereotypical of computer science (such as a Star Trek poster and video games) to objects not considered stereotypical of computer science (such as a nature poster and phone books – this was back in 2009, when we still used phone books!) was sufficient to boost female undergraduates' interest in computer science to the level of their male peers.[100]

There **are other supporting design** changes that can be done to **re-frame perceptions.** For example, two universities (Harvey Mudd University & Carnegie Mellon University) in the U. S. had less than 10% of women studying computer science. They both implemented targeted design changes ranging from **renaming** introductory computer science courses to signal skills such as 'creative problem solving' rather than programming language (like Java). They also set 'leadership skills' as part of the requirement to be a computer science major. Through these design changes and others integrated for wider systemic change, Maria Klawe, the president of Harvey Mudd University, said that they *"countered the stereotype that computer geeks were guys who spent all their time alone in a basement. They had very deliberately made it collaborative and involving teamwork instead of being lonely."*[101] Both universities have surpassed over 40% women studying computer science at their institutions. *Framing Perceptions* Inclusion Nudges can make a huge difference in terms of signaling what is valued, who is welcomed, and what is possible.

### Other design versions
Other global campaigns have been started similar to Isis' one. For example, two focused on other professions of physicists and surgeons. The BBC reported that in the first week, the surgeon hashtag appeared *"more than 12,000 times on Twitter. Women now account for around half of medical graduates in the UK, but just 11% of surgical consultants – and one study suggests that figure is rising by just 1% every four years. A paper written by a male surgeon, Ed Fitzgerald, found that in Britain, over half of male and two-thirds of female newly graduated doctors did not think surgery welcomed women."*[102]

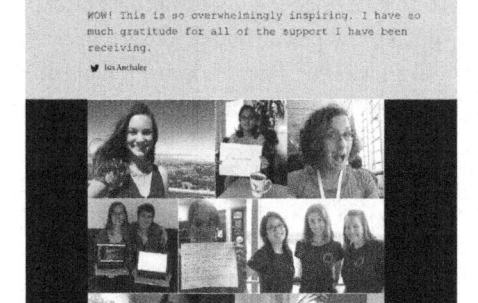

*Images from #ILOOKLIKEAN-
ENGINEER: ONE YEAR LATER.
Isis Anchalee, Medium,
3 August 2016*

We encourage you to consider how you can use inspiration from these kinds of campaigns and global movements in your communication style, messages, and materials about your organisation, community, initiative, etc. Attracting talent rarely happens with a only job advert. How could you counter stereotypes, engage diverse target groups, and humanise your image by showing real people?

## Publicly Available Resources

See **GoldieBlox's Fast-Forward Girls 2015** video that highlights **role models** and the #ILookLikeA… statements.
https://www.youtube.com/watch?v=Xy1Y_6M18vE

Photographer **Helena Price's** Techie project shares photos and stories of under-represented people in the technology sector to show *"a more comprehensive view of the people who work in tech"*.
https://techiesproject.com/

> **WHAT & HOW**
> I'll make sure to attract
> a diverse pool of candidates

Inclusive Evaluations & Decisions

# Structured Scoring of 6 Qualifications

## The Challenge

Even when we know that our intuitive judgements are often flawed, we tend to believe we can dismiss first impressions of people and rate their fit for a position solely based on facts about their attributes and merits. The challenge is how to make a structured fact-based evaluation free of bias, and still use our intuition. And how to ensure that we act in accordance with the evidence that *"simple statistical rules are superior to intuitive judgements"*?[103]

Anywhere you have to make evaluations and selections (of people, ideas, products, services, etc.), we need to make sure to de-bias the process. Nobel Laurate **Daniel Kahnman's** factual interviewing and structured scoring process[104] is a very impactful approach to mitigate intuitive judgements and improve the quality of the evaluation and decision. The founder and CEO of Applied, **Kate Glazebrook** and her team including **Diana Rocha** and **Andrew Babbage** have also shared a similar structured approach with us. We describe these below and have supplemented with other structured approaches.

> **The Inclusion Nudge**
>
> Evaluate candidates for a job based on 6 independent qualifications. Score each qualification separately on a 1-5 scale. Choose the candidate with the highest total score.

**Purpose:** Design the evaluation and selection processes for objectivity and reduction of influence of biases to focus on merits and potential.

## How To

See below on how you can make your own version. As you read through this, keep in mind that this Inclusion Nudge begins with identifying the qualification criteria for the position (now and in the future), and these should be the foundation for the job description, job advert, application process, interview guide, evaluation of the candidate, as well as the selection process.

### ❶ Prepare
### Version 1: Kahneman's identification of qualifications
Select 5 to 6 traits that are prerequisites for success in this position. Choose traits that are as independent from each other as possible (technical proficiency, reliability, communication, leadership, and so on). You have to be able to assess these separately and reliably by asking a few factual questions. Make a list of such factual questions for each trait.

Kahneman found that obtaining as much specific information as possible about the interviewee's life in the candidate's normal environment is the best predictor of a match to the job. Frame questions about the past and present; their interest in sports, activities, frequency of interactions with friends, how punctual they are in work and studies, etc. Do not make judgements about the candidate's future adjustment to the position.

### Version 2: Applied's work-scenario questions
Come up with 'the what': 5 to 7 things that a person needs to be able to do on the job and be specific. Convert these into work tests or scenario-based questions. You can use these as part of the application process, instead of a traditional application. A few examples are:

*"It's your first week on the job and you're new to the local area. You've been told that your first priority is to build relationships with the community. How do you spend the week?"*
(looks for interpersonal and stakeholder management skills)

*"Imagine you have an opportunity to pitch to work on the biggest challenge facing the public sector. What challenge do you choose and why?"*
(looks for strategic thinking and public sector understanding/interest)

The team at Applied has found that work-related tests have the highest predictive validity. Applied recommends telling the interviewees upfront that you'll be taking them through a structured interview based on the scenario-based questions which could feel a little wooden, but that it's designed to help them shine.

### ❷ Interview and evaluation (in both versions 1 and 2)

Collect the information on one trait at a time. Keep the same order of questions in all interview to ensure candidates aren't unfairly discouraged when one question/task is more challenging than others. This will also help with comparison.

Scoring immediately and individually reduces judgmental errors. Try to do it as you go, or at least as soon as you can when the candidate leaves. You can help yourself by always leaving time between candidates to score. Scoring each trait before you move on to the next one. Do not skip around. Score on a scale of 1 (weak) to 5 (strong), or however score ordering happens in your culture.

Make sure each of the members in the recruitment panel make the rating by themselves before sharing with each other to avoid group conformity.

### ❸ Selection (in both versions 1 and 2)

Add up the scores and select the person with the highest score (even if you like another candidate better).

Use a template for this, because it gives an option to rate the traits in batches for each candidate.

Review trait 1 for all, then trait 2 for all, and so on. This way you avoid rating based on comparison to stereotypes.

Create a template by adding the names of the candidates (vertical columns), and the traits (horizontal rows) after all the interviews and scoring is done. See an illustration on the next page.

**EXAMPLE** STRUCTURE AND SELECT THE ONE WITH THE HIGHEST TOTAL

| Screening criteria<br>Traits/qualifications<br>SCORE 1-5 | Candidate A | Candidate B | Candidate C | Candidate D | Candidate E |
|---|---|---|---|---|---|
| 1. Technical proficiency<br>Factual questions | 2 | 2 | 4 | 5 | 3 |
| 2. People development<br>Factual questions | 1 | 2 | 4 | 5 | 3 |
| 3. Participatory decision making<br>Factual questions | 5 | 5 | 5 | 4 | 5 |
| 4. Xxxxxxx<br>Factual questions | 4 | 3 | 4 | 2 | 3 |
| 5. XXX<br>Factual questions | 5 | 5 | 5 | 3 | 4 |
| **TOTAL** | 17 | 17 | (22) | 19 | 18 |

*The template and image created by Tinna C. Nielsen*

## Impact

**Kahneman** tested this method when he was working in the Israeli Defence Forces early in his career and set up an interview system for assessing the personality of soldiers to make the right match with various positions.

The procedure improved the outcome from previous interviews where intuition had been dominating. The sum of the rating system predicted soldiers' performance much more accurately (not perfect, but much better).

**Kahneman** and the interviewers also used a version that added intuitive judgement. After the rating of the candidate, the interviewers would close their eyes and imaging the candidate as a soldier, and this also turned out to add value. But it only had an impact after the disciplined collection of objective information and structured scoring of separate traits. The lesson learned was do not trust intuition but do not dismiss it either.

The team at **Applied** is in the process of testing all of these elements as part of their technology-based solution. Part of this is also testing the impact of one-on-one interviews versus panel interviews based on research suggesting that successive interviews with different members of the team are better than panel interviews. This is largely because they mitigate the risk of **groupthink** on the part of the reviewers. More contact is probably also better for getting a representative sample of the candidate. And if you do multiple interviews, you can shuffle the order of who sees whom and when, allowing you to mitigate **ordering bias** that can influence scores (like being more generous to the first few, or kinder after a terrible interview).

## Authors' Comments & Behavioural Insights

### Why it works: behavioural insights

This approach works because it mitigates the **'halo effect' bias** that influences any kind of evaluation of people (such as letting one small positive experience spill over into our overall evaluation). Extensive research shows that halo effects are most likely to occur when people employ rapid, automatic processing (system 1) but it disappears when processing more deliberatively (system 2). This is consistent in various everyday situations.

Research findings also show how good or bad **moods** can influence people's tendency to rely on irrelevant information when **forming impressions**. Positive moods increase halo effects and negative moods promoted a more **systematic processing style** which eliminated halo effects.[105] With this structured approach, we can avoid that mood influence.

Scoring each part separately is critical to improving accuracy and objectivity. Beside mitigating the halo effect, it also helps avoid the **peak-end effect**, which predisposes us to remember the peak and the end of an experience and brushes over the rest of experiences. We are less likely to recall the collective experience or the other moments beyond the peak and the ending.

We encourage you try out various versions of this. As we have experienced many times when experimenting with this kind of structured scoring approach, it is always a surprise to realise how different the members in a recruitment committee perceive and rate the candidates. These differences have given some fascinating insights about each other, created curious conversations when exploring each other's views and perceptions, and thus given ground to get to know each other better. This has always strengthened inclusive collaboration in the group. Without doubt, this is important for making inclusive talent selection. Give it a try.

Inclusive Evaluations & Decisions

# Anonymise People to Focus on Merit

## The Challenge

Often, the screening and evaluation process for a new hire or promotion is influenced by such visual impressions as the layout and style of a resume or application, as well as by implicit associations of gender, skin colour, age, and other biases. This is also the case in the analysis of assessment results, in interviews, and in the selection processes. To ensure a fair process and selection of the best candidates, it is crucial to design the process to be as objective as possible.

Unconscious bias awareness and intercultural intelligence are not enough to make the screening and selection process objective. It is necessary to implement steps that help the brain make better decisions and reduce the negative impact of biases, and thus challenge the behavioural drivers of the status quo, mindless choice, and confirmation bias.

> **The Inclusion Nudge**
>
> Make candidates anonymous in the evaluation and selection process by removing as much identity data as possible in applications.

**Purpose:** Ensure a focus on merit and qualifications by removing visual and identity information that may trigger bias and detract from objective decision making in various stages within a talent selection process.

## How To

There are different opportunities to integrate this intervention as part of existing talent attraction and hiring processes and systems. Some of these are described below.

The process can be fully automated, such as in this example.

→ In the recruiting technology-based system, demographic identity factors, such as gender, age, name, address, and photo, are not revealed to the recruiter and the interviewing team during the early screening process steps.

→ Only when the candidates for interviewing have been selected is identity information given, if at all as in some cases the identify data still may not be given then depending on other bias mitigating design steps in the full talent attraction process.

The process design can also be fully manual, such as it was done in this example. When resumes come in, have an assistant manually remove names and geographic information, assigning each resume a number. This is how many hiring managers did it in Arla Foods where **Tinna C. Nielsen** was the Global Head of Inclusion. They came up with this themselves after having experienced a *Feel the Need* Inclusion Nudge. Also, at a Danish film institute, when Tinna worked with the reviewers of applications for film funding, they asked their assistant to cut out all identity data from paper versions of the applications.

→ Let the applicants know about this process design. Write on your talent attraction website, application platform, and in the job description that applicants should remove identity data from the application and CV and submit a separate page with this information.

→ Instruct your assistant or colleague to hold onto the separate identity page. You request it when you have chosen the candidates you want to meet for an interview. **Tinna** does this in her organisation Move the Elephant for Inclusiveness. Also, we noticed on **Stephen Frost's** (CEO of Frost Included and a contributor to *The Inclusion Nudges Guidebook*) company website that they have done this in past job postings.

## Many ways you can do this
### Anonymise internally
You can also anonymise when selecting members for internal councils, communities, panels, etc. In a technology firm in Denmark it was decided to build an internal community of champions to master and spread the Inclusion Nudges change techniques in their organisation. The (former) CEO was to select a diverse group of 12 leaders in the organisation based on their application to be part of this community. **Ulla Dalsgaard** (one of the Diversity Leads) gave him a list of 50 applicants without any identity data (anonymous). The CEO said *"How am I supposed to choose when I cannot see who they are?"*. As soon as he had said that, he realised that this was exactly why he needed help with selecting the team objectively and not in a biased manner.

### Blind skills assessments
**Kedar Iyer**, from the organisation GapJumpers, shared that they worked with a technology company to apply blind skills assessments (anonymising the candidates' assessment results) for specific roles in their talent attraction process. Anonymising the candidate on the CV is not enough based on some research findings[106] and GapJumpers' experience. Instead, their focus is on the assessment testing and results reporting to be anonymised within the talent attraction process.

### Request anonymised shortlist of search agency
Another option is when you use search agencies to help you find candidates, and you ask them to deliver a list of diverse candidates, remember to require (make this part of your formal contractual agreement) of them to anonymise candidates on both the long- and short-lists. **Lisa Kepinski** (Founder of Inclusion Institute) did this when she was an internal head of inclusion and diversity in a multinational. This was a two-step process. First, it was necessary to set the contracted terms that the search agency would deliver gender diverse candidates (the percentage target varied based on the role and function, such as at least 30% females for IT and 50% for finance). Only a few people had visibility to verify that the list met the agreed upon targets. Secondly, when presenting these to the recruiting lead and hiring manager, the candidate list and information was anonymised.

## Impact

The impact of the various ways of anonymising candidates are more diversity in the final pool of qualified candidates. This is due to a more objective process, which thus creates a better chance of selecting the best qualified candidate and achieving more diversity. In all the organisations where **Lisa Kepinski** and **Tinna C. Nielsen** have worked and helped redesign their talent selection processes, every person having applied this anonymising approach has expressed the similiar insight and change. They tell us comments such as, "We always end up selecting a person whom at first impression we wouldn't have considered if the anonymising process design wasn't used."

What **Ulla** did was to apply the anonymised screening Inclusion Nudge to help them to choose objectively from the list of candidates according to the qualification criteria. She had also helped the CEO realise the importance of anonymising the applicants and *feel the need* to make this change in the selection process.

This internal community was diverse in terms of gender, tenure, age, function, and professional background. They went through a full Inclusion Nudge Design Learning Lab with **Tinna.** The community has since been assigned several corporate tasks by the executive team and additionally other teams in the organisation are asking for their assistance.

**Kedar** shared that in an organisation that they worked with the anonymised skills assessment resulted in 20 % more minority candidates selected to interview for software engineering roles and 32 % more minority candidates selected for data analytics roles. The process also included candidates from more diverse backgrounds than the established norm, with 40 % of those selected for interviews being self-taught and/or educated at boot camps rather than the traditional university education path. This 'alternative' education path had not previously been a criterion to advance in the talent selection process. They also found that the blind skills assessments reduced the total time to hire by 26 %. So, not only was the talent pool more diverse and the process fairer, but it was also more efficient.

In **Lisa's** example, there were two key learnings from the experience. The first was that a level of oversight was needed to ensure that the search agency actually delivered on the expectation for a gender diverse list. It was hard for them to shift their past ways of sourcing candidates. At that time, her organisation was one of the search firm's very few clients that *required* this of them. Other clients talked about wanting it, but did not put in place serious contract targets for them to deliver on it. Their first results with Lisa's organisation didn't match up to their expectation. This is why a step of having an internal reviewer of the candidate lists (Lisa and/or a member of the talent attraction team not involved in filling the role) was put in place before going onward in the process. Initially, this review happened with every list, and later it fell to spot checks after the search agency improved to meet the expectations (contractual agreements). Another learning was that often the search consultant would present the lists in two formats, one written and then a briefing discussion with the hiring manager. The latter allowed for the influence of bias by how the search consultant referenced some candidates over others. While the process design of having the candidate list anonymised was working, the next step in the process skewed the hiring manager's decision making. So, they eliminated the briefing discussion and only used the written lists. There was an increase in women who were interviewed after this process was put in place.

Another example of this design having impact is from a technology & engineering multinational (who shares this anonymously). They applied the approach in selecting members for their internal Diversity, Equity, and Inclusion (DEI) Council in the U.S., after having read about it in the past edition of *The Inclusion Nudges Guidebook*. They were surprised, and pleased, with the unexpected results of who was selected to serve on their DEI Council. This *Process Design* Inclusion Nudge bought in wider diversity than they had anticipated and was a reminder of how their own views could have influenced who was not considered if they hadn't put the anonymous process in place.

## Authors' Comments & Behavioural Insights

### Why it works: behavioural insights

Anonymising people works because it avoids the **halo effect** to influence the evaluation of a person's merit. The halo effect is an error in reasoning based on one single trait, often irrelevant, that creates a 'halo' of the overall impression and perception of that person.[107]

The term halo effect was coined in 1920 by psychologist Edward L. Thorndike. It's based on Thorndike's observations of military officers 'ranking' of subordinates. Before communicating with their subordinates, the officers ranked them based on character traits, which included leadership ability and intelligence. Their **positive and negative perceptions** were based on unrelated traits that had to do with physical impressions. For example, a tall and attractive subordinate was perceived as being the most intelligent. He was also ranked as overall 'better' than the others. Thorndike found that **physical appearances** are the most influential in determining our overall impressions of another person's character, which can result in either positive or negative perceptions. The halo bias can have negative consequences on your ability to think critically about a person's other traits and abilities.

The halo effect does not only influence evaluation and selection in hiring situations, but also when it comes to ideas, investments, pitching, and also in schools. For example, there's some evidence that perceived attractiveness can lead to higher grades in school.[108] Another study found that teachers assigned higher grades to the essays by students with **common, popular, and attractive first names** versus essays by students with rare, unpopular, and unattractive names.[109]

### A need for a whole system de-biasing process

There is a compelling need to design to reduce the influence of bias within your processes across the whole system, not just one part of the system, such as only with recruiting by anonymising applicants.

This was illustrated by the recent discrimination legal case with the Boston symphony orchestra. They were one of the first institutions to implement anonymous interviewing decades ago, by implementing anonymous music auditions behind a screen and as a result increasing the number of women by 40% and also changing the ethnic make up of the orchestra. Yet, they were sued by a leading female member of the Philharmonic for being significantly underpaid (the case was for more than $200,000 in unpaid wages) to her male counterparts in the orchestra. This was because the Boston symphony had not ensured that its whole system had been redesigned to lessen bias effects. Further reports have shown that while now women comprise about 47% of musicians in symphony orchestras in the U.S., there are very few female composers who have their music performed by symphony orchestras in the U.S. During the 2019-20 season in the U.S., 90% of the music to be played is from male composers and only 10% from women composers, with *"the numbers for composer of color even more dismal"*.[110]

Designing to reduce bias needs to happen across all processes that work within the whole system. When you are implementing this example, look at the connected processes across the total organisation and apply the same de-biasing and nudge design approach.

**Inclusive Evaluations & Decisions**

# Default as 'All Qualified' & 'Why Not'

## The Challenge

**?** This is an Inclusion Nudge that is a very simple design with big impact. This illustrates how easy it can be for all of us to be more inclusive. Here are two examples of how people have applied it with significant influence to address the challenge of biased talent selections.

Mental shortcuts and biases can work against making good evaluations and decisions about people, solutions, ideas, roles, and much more. Often this is due to the starting point (the default and the anchor) of that process. The challenge is that qualified, sometimes even the best, solutions and people are de-selected. When it comes to talent evaluations in organisations, this is critical because it has a significant influence on the successful achievement of the organisations's strategy and purpose. Yet, bias impacts evaluation of performance with a tendency to rating recent performance more highly than past performance. People tend to opt-in on people who fit the implicit norms and have similarities to themselves. They reflect the status quo and so feel safer.

**Sue Johnson**, who was then the global head of diversity & inclusion at Nestlé, noticed a pattern in her past company during talent discussions. People who were seen as different from the norms, who were also usually the same people labelled as 'diverse', were talked about as *"Should we take a risk on this person?"* or *"Is this person a safe bet?"*. These people were often not similar to the decision makers or deviated from the implicit norm and stereotypes of the 'typical' employee for that role. This resulted in unequal evaluations, and thus unequal opportunities for career opportunities, compensation, and a loss of performance potential in the organisation. Sue implemented a simple change in the process design to shift the default of the discussions.

At the University of Copenhagen, Professor and Deputy Head of the Mathematical Sciences Department **Tinne Hoff Kjeldsen** 🧠 and Professor and Head of Mathematical Sciences Department, **Michael Sørensen** 🧠 had to find a new Head of Studies internally among the tenured staff. This is an important role but a role that no one is eager to take on. This is because it's time consuming and takes time away from doing research and teaching, which is what their performance is evaluated on and determines their next career opportunities. Tinne and Michael decided to split up the role in smaller functions and invited all to apply, but no one did. They then did as they normally did, they asked the same people as they always asked to take on additional similar functions and assignment. But they all had legitimate reasons for declining. The department was stuck. Based on participating in a co-creation process of redesigning their recruitment process by applying the Inclusion Nudges change approach, Tinne and Michael found inspiration from this default design.

> **The Inclusion Nudge**
>
> Make the default in evaluations and selection processes
> "All are qualified".
>
> Change the argumentation default to
> "Why not?"

**Purpose:** Shift the anchor of the thought process to promote more objective evaluations and work against biased tendencies in decision making. In most organisations, when deciding who to select for a project or promotion, leaders ask, *"Who is qualified?"* and then, they argue *"Why?"* the candidates they find more qualified are ready. That is a very biased process. With a default of *"All are qualified"*, they have to argue *"Why not?"* (opt out) instead of *"Why?"* (opt in).

## How To

Implement this in successor evaluation meetings *('All are qualified')* or performance-calibration meetings *('All start with the highest rating').*

When it comes to people, for example when evaluating each candidate for a job, it's important to search for facts about why this person would not be qualified and why this person would be qualified. Make sure the evaluators challenge each other on the assumptions about the candidates. Make it fact based.

→ Make a list of all candidates (all people in the team, department, level, tenure, talent program, etc.).

→ Discuss each candidate on the list by arguing based on facts. Address these questions: *"Why would this person not be qualified?"* and *"Why would this person be qualified?"*

→ In the decision process, compare the candidates and arguments to make sure, you don't compare to a stereotype, but merits and facts.

This is how they applied this default design in the evaluation and selection process for the Head of Studies at the Department of Mathematics. Tinne Hoff Kjeldsen explains *"When no one volunteered to take on the role and everyone we found qualified declined our invitation to take the role, we decided to use a much more systematic approach and change the default from 'opt in' to 'opt out' in our evaluation of who were qualified. This way we broaden our pool of candidates. We made a list of all people (at the level and with the experience needed) and systematically discussed each of them 'why not' and 'why'. This broadened our outlook and we found several other candidates than those we had asked."*

Apply this default in idea pitching processes, innovation processes, hiring and promotion, and any where else where you have several options to choose from.

## Impact

Nestlé used this *Process Design* Inclusion Nudge to focus on promoting gender balance in succession planning. They changed the default in discussion about who was ready for a promotion or bigger responsibility to 'All are ready now'. This broadened the pool of candidates being evaluated, it shifted the perspective on what it means to be ready, reduced bias in the decision-making process, and promoted more objective evaluations.

At the University of Copenhagen, this Inclusion Nudge changed the view of who was qualified to take on the various functions. Starting from not finding a single person, by applying this design they found several qualified people to take on the various functions and they all accepted the offer. This is how Tinne and Michael described the impact; *"The design turned out to work really well for us in this situation and to solve our challenge. We will most likely try this out in other situations. The strength of this approach is that everybody is included. This does not guarantee that we do not overlook some people but at least everybody is taken into consideration from the beginning."*

## Authors' Comments & Behavioural Insights

We believe that this kind of default design has the potential to reduce biases about nationality, race, ethnicity, gender identity, sexual orientation, abilities, personality, communication style, age, etc., thereby increasing diversity broadly in leadership and talent pipelines.

We also see that this can be applied to other decision-making processes to ensure that a more open perspective is activated rather than a limiting one driven by our mental fallacies and biases. For example, in idea pitching sessions for funding, investors, and internal resource allocation.

### Why it works: behavioural insights

Changing the **default** has been used in many situations with positive effects and multiple outcomes.

One well-known example is with organ donation programmes shifting the **default** from citizens having to register **(opt in)** to a default where all citizens are registered and free to **opt out.** In the countries where people have to opt in, very few people register despite their intentions to do so (it's too complex a choice and too effortful). In the countries where the default is automatic registration the majority of citizens stay in the system. This works because it **reduces complexity** and makes it **effortless** to do what we intend to do. Very few people *opt out* because that is an equally complex choice and as effortful as *opting in*.

Using **default** nudges to foster more inclusion, changes our thinking from an unconscious choice based on bias to a conscious search for facts. Selecting the best qualified candidates requires that we view a diverse pool of candidates, but most people have difficulty opting in on diversity, such as a person who is not like the majority, does not fit the implicit norms in the organisation, is a minority, does not look or communicate like those already working in that position, etc. This requires more effort and involves complexity in choosing. **Opting in on someone we do not recognise as a 'fit' is difficult. On the other hand, *opting out* on a qualified candidate (when having facts that counter bias) is an equally difficult process even when they don't fit the norm.**

With the *'all are qualified'* **default** we make sure it does not require a lot of effort to opt in on **'outliers'** (those perceived as having some form of difference from the norm) and we make it less likely that they are going to opt out on a qualified candidate due to diversity or not an obvious cultural 'fit'. This will help ensure the best qualified and more diversity is selected.

Inclusive Evaluations & Decisions

# Ask Flip Questions to Change Your Perceptions in the Moment

## The Challenge

It can be difficult to see how biases affect us and it's almost impossible to be consciously aware of our unconscious reactions in the moment as we are interacting with other people. As individuals we hold many unconscious biases about other people. Since these are often hidden to us and also sometimes work against our own intentions and self-perception as fair, bias plays out in micro-behaviours that result in a waste of human resources and inequality. The challenge is how to avoid that our biases negatively influence the way we perceive, judge, evaluate, listen, talk, and behave, thus affect our selection of talent. How can we challenge our biases in our interactions with other people when we can't control them and it is too difficult to be aware of all our biases? And more importantly, how do we change our perceptions and behaviour in the moment, in the situation as we evaluate applications, make performance reviews, and interview candidates?

**Tinna C. Nielsen,** Founder of Move the Elephant for Inclusiveness, and **Lisa Kepinski,** Founder of Inclusion Institute, have used what we call "Flip Questions" for over a decade to change this and we still do this. Our biases do not disappear just because we know a lot about bias. Here is how we do it.

## The Inclusion Nudge

Ask Flip Questions silently to yourself – in your head as you are in the moment – as you are interacting with people.

Here are a few examples:

*"If she had been a man, would I have responded differently to what she just did?"*

or

*"If he was not 25 years old, but had 25 years more experience than me, would I have listened differently to what he just said?"*

**Purpose:** Flip and counter your immediate perception (bias, stereotypes, preconception) in the moment of interaction. It's about creating a trigger in our body to realise our own biased thinking. This can help us change our unconscious thought processes and change our behaviours in the moment.

## How To

You ask the questions silently to yourself – in your head, but you can also ask them out loud to other people and groups of people to help them reflect and see from another perspective. Ask yourself Flip Question as you are interacting with people, such as listening to them talk or share an idea or give a presentation or during job interviews or other situations. Where there are people, there are biases, so Flip Questions are relevant to apply everywhere.

### How to design Flip Questions

You start the question with *"If ..."* and then you frame a question based on some of the visible characteristics of the other person or some insights you have about your own biases or some insights from surveys or other sources about specific biases or stereotypes. When framing the question, the aim is to find the opposite perspective. Check out these examples for inspiration.

Let's use height as an example of how bias can influence us in many ways, and how you can frame a variety of Flip Questions to counter this. If you know you have a positive bias towards tall people (perhaps because you are tall yourself or because you are influenced by the stereotype that tall people are an authority) then counter that bias by asking yourself Flip Questions such as these below.

*"If he/she was NOT tall like me, would I then ask more critical questions?"* or

*"If he was not so short, would I think he was more competent?"* or

*"If she/he was not the tallest candidate, would I ask different kinds of questions right now?"*

If you know the data (from research)[111] about the tallest candidates being selected for leadership positions, then most people want to make sure that kind of bias does not influence their evaluation of the candidate's merit and their decision about who to hire for a leadership position. To counter this, you can ask yourself Flip Questions, such as the suggested examples above, and you can also supplement Flip Questions with a couple of questions to highlight the absurdity of bias. Adding a bit of playfulness to the seriousness of the situation has also proven to be effective in changing our perception. Here are a couple of examples below.

*"Are tall people better leaders because they are tall?"* or

*"Are tall people better at executing on strategy because they have long legs and are taller than the others?"*

## Inspiration to design your Flip Questions

- *If she was a man and not a woman, would I interpret her as frustrated instead of hysterical as I just did?*

- *If he was slim and not overweight, would I perceive what he just said as more credible?*

- *If she was smiling more, would I find her more likable?*

- *If he was less aggressive, would I ask more critical questions?*

- *If the pitch of his voice was deeper and not so high, would I listen more to the content of what he is saying?*

- *If she did not have a disability, would I speak so slowly and loud to her?*

- *If he did not have a dark skin colour, would I feel less sceptical?*

- *If he had not been positioned as an expert by the CEO, would I then speak up with my knowledge about the flaws in his data?*

- *If she was less introvert in her communication style, would I listen more interested and passionate?*

- *If she was less extrovert and loud in her presentation style, would I listen more to the content of her presentation?*

- *If she was a man, what salary would I offer him?*

- *If he wore a suit, would I have seen him as a better leader?*

- *If this candidate did not graduate from the same school as me, would I have said they were as well-prepared?*

- *If his tattoo was not visible, would I have felt safer around him?*

- *If her hair weren't grey, would I have viewed her as more agile and innovative at work?*

- *If I say 'yes' to this request, then what am I saying 'no' to?*

- *If she didn't have children, would I have considered her for this international assignment?*

**There are no limitations for what kind of Flip Questions you can ask. Remember to also ask Flip Questions to other people and groups you work with.**

### Online design version

This *Framing Perceptions* Inclusion Nudge is as relevant to use in online and telephone interactions as in-person. Biases are also triggered by hearing a voice, the pitch of the voice, and the speed of talking.

You can make a little experiment with yourself; if you cannot see how people look in the online setting, then look them up afterwards to see how they look and pay attention to what kind of perceptions your mind made up – often you'll be surprised. Based on these new insights you can make some great Flip Questions. Give it a try.

## Impact

In our work as change makers, Lisa and Tinna have trained and enabled thousands of people worldwide in how to make and use Flip Questions. Of all the enablers we spread, this simple technique is the one most people apply in their daily interactions and in their evaluation and decision-making processes. When it's possible for us to follow up to measure how many use Flip Questions is been 70-80 %. We always encourage people to write down their Flip Question (this improves memory) and also to share them with each other. In our sessions, they write them on sticky notes and make a poster with all their examples, so they can learn from reading each other's.

The impact of asking Flip Questions to yourself is obvious when you ask them, because whenever you can answer *'yes'* to your questions, you will often experience some kind of trigger. It can be an emotional trigger, such as surprise or annoyance, or it can be a physical trigger where you feel some reaction in your body, for example in your stomach or your pulse increases. These triggers are your enablers to change your perception and react and behave differently in the moment instead of blindly following your unconscious instinct.

## Authors' Comments & Behavioural Insights

We have asked ourselves Flip Questions for decades and it has become obvious to us that this kind of Flip Question will always be necessary to ask because regardless of our knowledge about bias and our expertise about how to mitigate bias, our biases continuously play out in our daily interactions.

Over the years we have been practicing self-compassion because answering Flip Questions is like holding up a mirror in front of yourself and you see things you didn't know about yourself. And the worst thing to do, is to blame yourself for being pre-judging and beat yourself up mentally. As shame researcher Brené Brown states, if you allow shame or denial to take control, then your mind will close down for learning, curiosity, and change. So, instead embrace what you see, make a positive reframing by praising that you noticed your bias and that you get a chance to change your perception and behaviour in the moment. *Embrace it – then you can change it.* We also ask many Flip Questions to other people and the result is always new reflections, interesting conversations about stereotypes, implicit norms, and un-reflected patterns of judgement.

### Why it works: behavioural insights

Flip Questions work because they **function as triggers** that help us see something that we are blind to and shift perceptions in the moment. When **seeing and feeling** our own biased thinking, it can help us change our unconscious thought processes and our behaviour, in the moment. That way our biases are not running the show. We need to combat the common notion that by simply being aware of our biases, then this can change them from influencing our behaviours and decision making. We need to help our own brain change perception in the moment. Flipping perspective is an effective way to ensure detachment to maintain objectivity in evaluating people, issues, and perspectives. **Detachment** means the ability to step back to see the bigger picture and act on it.

## Publicly Available Resources

You can learn more about Flip Questions and some of **Tinna C. Nielsen's** personal stereotypes in her **TEDx Talk** *Nudge Behaviour for A More Inclusive World*
https://www.youtube.com/watch?v=VggAqa0xOwM

Inclusive Evaluations & Decisions

# No CV Application to Reduce Biased Evaluation

## The Challenge

The evidence shows that CVs are a pretty poor predictor of job performance[112] and the way in which organisations review applications can be a source of different sorts of biases that impede selecting the best talent and building more diverse teams. **Kate Glazebrook**, the CEO at the organisation Applied and members of her team, including **Andrew Babbage** and **Diana Rocha**, designed these solutions to address challenges that can be part of the application reviews during the hiring process.

### The Inclusion Nudge

Here are 2 examples:

No CVs. Instead, applicants submit three to five 250-word limit answers to job preview questions.

Evaluations are done by using several behavioural interventions: anonymise, chunking, randomising, and crowdsourcing (described in detail below).

**Purpose:** Increase objectivity and remove the influence of any potential biases when considering applications and making hiring decisions.

## How To

The principles that are applied during the submission, allocation, scoring, and shortlisting of applications are described below.

### ❶ Application submission

Instead of CVs, candidates submit three to five 250-word limit answers to job preview questions. These questions test a combination of job knowledge and situational judgement. They are most effective when covering types of skills and work that accurately reflect the job itself.

Here are some examples of questions:

*"It's your first week on the job and you're new to the local area. You've been told that your first priority is to build relationships with the community. How do you spend the week?"*
[This question looks for interpersonal and stakeholder management skills.]

*"Imagine you have an opportunity to pitch to work on the biggest challenge facing the public sector. What challenge do you choose and why?"*
[This question looks for strategic thinking and public sector understanding and interest.]

### ❷ Allocation and scoring

Allocating answers works like allocation of cards to different members of the hiring team. Each answer/card can be scored from 1 to 5. The principles that underlie this allocation and scoring are the following.

#### Anonymise
Remove names and all candidate personal details so hiring teams just focus on answers.

#### Chunk
Instead of reviewing a candidate's application in full vertically, hiring teams do direct, horizontal comparisons of candidates - reviewing a batch of answers to question 1, then to question 2, and so on.

**Randomise**
Randomise the order of all the candidate responses. That way, no candidate is disproportionately advantaged or disadvantaged by where they show up in the pile.

**Crowdsource**
Allow to gather views from multiple members of a team simultaneously, so that a candidate's overall score is a more holistic measure of their quality. This is done independently, so no-one's affected by anyone else's perspectives.

### ❸ Shortlisting
Shortlisting is based on the average scores that candidates receive which makes the hiring process more transparent. Candidates who are shortlisted can go through a structured interview process. Candidates who do not meet a threshold, and therefore are not shortlisted, can receive a feedback link that summarises their performance against the average group and the best score.

## Impact

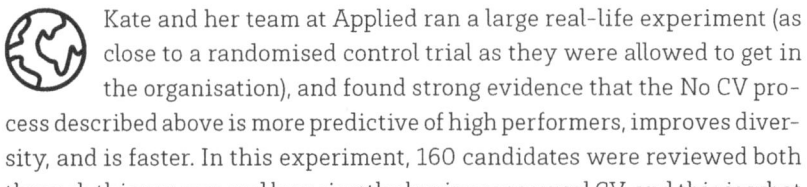

Kate and her team at Applied ran a large real-life experiment (as close to a randomised control trial as they were allowed to get in the organisation), and found strong evidence that the No CV process described above is more predictive of high performers, improves diversity, and is faster. In this experiment, 160 candidates were reviewed both through this process and by using the business as usual CV, and this is what they found.

**Smarter decisions**
60% of the candidates who were offered jobs wouldn't have been hired if they had relied on their CVs alone. Candidates who scored better through the No CV process also had a high score in the two in-person rounds. In contrast, there was no discernible correlation between their CV score and their performance in those later rounds.

**More diverse teams**
The No CV process made for a fairer process, relative to traditional CV sifting, and was especially good for promoting social mobility based on educational background. It was less negatively biased against people from backgrounds

other than White and with a disability. Statistical evidence was also found in terms of educational background. On average, candidates had a wider array of attainment levels, whereas it looked like the CV sift was much more focused on attainment as a metric.

**Faster recruitment processes**
The process saved around 30 minutes on each candidate. More importantly, time was spent much more intelligently, with 75 % of the time spent on reviewing candidates. While in contrast, 61 % of the time using the CV sift was spent on administration (from printing and collating hundreds of pieces of paper, to inputting scores back into spreadsheets, etc.).

## Authors' Comments & Behavioural Insights

Like with the *Process Design* Inclusion Nudge called **ANOMYMISE PEOPLE TO FOCUS ON MERIT** (→ page 131), both organisations of GapJumpers and Applied have reported not only more diversity in the candidates and better decision making, but also a speedier recruitment process. Given that both companies are offering technology-based solutions, it makes the process faster.

However, these are probably not the benefits that you are likely to achieve when you are doing it manually. Perhaps your own internal IT department can help to implement some de-biasing process efficiencies. And if you are doing it manually and see diversity, quality of decision making, and speed increase, please write us so we can update this example. We'd really like to hear about your solutions and results, as well.

### Why it works: behavioural insights
Names and other socio-demographic details can be distracting and result in inadvertent bias (for example **affinity bias** or **stereotype bias**).

It's hard to simultaneously compare candidates in multiple areas at once, and that leads to cognitive overload (one of the triggers for bias). Reviewing candidates top to bottom also means we can fall prey to the **halo effect,** where if a candidate starts off strong (or weak), that affects everything we read and evaluate thereafter.

Our brains are heavily affected by **ordering effects** and small contextual factors around us. We tend to be kinder to those at the beginning or those just after a poor response. If we're hungry or tired, our scores are less reliable. All of this leads to 'noise' in the reviews, and a lack of objectivity.

People all have a slightly different way of seeing the world, and that means we rarely totally agree on what 'best qualified' is. When hiring decisions are left to one person, it can end up being skewed by their personal perspective. Alternatively, hiring decisions made in an open committee can result in **groupthink** or **social hierarchy biases** where our true opinions don't surface.

We recommend you read the Inclusion Nudge examples **CHUNK TO DEBUNK BIAS USING JOINT EVALUATIONS** (→ page 154), by Harvard Professor Iris Bohnet and **STRUCTURED SCORING OF 6 QUALIFICATIONS** (→ page 126) based on Nobel Laurate Daniel Kahneman's and Applied's experiences.

Inclusive Evaluations & Decisions

# Chunk to Debunk Bias Using Joint Evaluations

### The Challenge

When making decisions about people, we tend to compare to stereotypes rather than compare with other people and their performance. This is what **Iris Bohnet** ✊, Professor of Business & Government and Co-director of the Women & Public Policy Program at Harvard University, and her **research team** ✊ found in their studies.

Also, when it comes to evaluating merit, competencies, and potential in a selection or evaluation process, this is rarely objective and fact-based. It is often biased and based on stereotypes. In their research, they found that this changes when evaluating people in bundles instead of individually. Here is how they offer to do this.

### The Inclusion Nudge

Make joint evaluations of candidates a part of the recruitment, promotion, and/or performance calibration processes instead of individual evaluations which are traditionally used.

**Purpose:** Joint evaluations replace stereotyped reference points with instead a reference point based on comparison to the other candidates and their merit. This focuses the assessment on the skills needed for the job and who is the best qualified candidate. This design ensures the evaluation process is less likely to trigger automatic associations or biases. It affects with whom candidates are compared, and thus, how competent they are perceived, rated, and who is ultimately selected.

## How To

To ensure we meet our intentions of fairness, objectivity, and good decision making, we need to reduce cognitive overload and interference of implicit associations. Here are some ways to do it in a promotion process.

### ❶ Standard promotion decisions

Require supervisors to recommend at least two people for consideration for promotion to force them to evaluate their pool comparatively rather than only someone whom they are most familiar. Have a promotion committee evaluate all suggested candidates comparatively, focusing on performance criteria that are as objective as possible. Be aware that gender bias tends to be particularly pronounced not when evaluating people based on past performance but rather when judging their future potential.

### ❷ One-off promotion decisions, for example to counter an outside offer

If you do not have the luxury of evaluating various candidates simultaneously but have to respond to market pressures, then trigger different references in the evaluators' minds by sharing a sample of people who have recently been promoted to the level under consideration. Include some **counter-stereotypical examples** to avoid automatic comparisons with the 'ideal' or typical person which is a biased implicit norm.

## Impact

People conducting joint evaluations are much more likely to choose candidates based on their past performance and not their gender bias. In separate evaluations, they are more likely to choose candidates based on their gender.

See more on Professor Iris Bohnet's research in *When Performance Trumps Gender Bias: Joint Versus Separate Evaluation* and in *What Works*.

## Authors' Comments & Behavioural Insights

As long-time change makers for inclusion, we, **Tinna Nielsen,** Founder of Move the Elephant for Inclusiveness, and **Lisa Kepinski,** Founder of Inclusion Institute, suggest that in addition to promotions, this can also be applied to the hiring process. By tapping into the decision-making reference point through a technique of chunking or grouping candidates, the outcome of selecting the most qualified can be better achieved.

**For hiring interviews, chunk assessment information**
Define the minimum (5 or less) competencies that are 'must have's' for the role. Then, design one interview question per competency that will allow the candidates to demonstrate their skills based on past experience. Ask all candidates the same set of questions during their interviews. Post interviews, when the hiring panel members share their notes and ratings from the interviews with each other and the hiring manager, they all use a process of not talking about the impressions of person by person (such as *'OK, what did you think about Pat?'*), but instead go through the information jointly, in **competency chunks.** Such as, first discuss all the response ratings from all candidates to Competency Question #1, then to Competency Question #2, and so on. This helps to focus on the actual competencies' assessment and not the person (and potentially activating stereotypes and biases about the person).

### Why it works: behavioural insights
This format of jointly sharing interview feedback by job competencies helps to focus the thinking and discussion on the required role needs already identified as 'must have's'. It helps decision making to be in alignment with the intention of hiring based on what is needed for the position. It also helps to reduce distracting personal **identity aspects** that can be more impacted by bias and **stereotypes** (such as *'Did you know that Pat is ...?'*).

By grouping, the relevant competencies and ratings, it's easier to process and **mental overload** is less likely to trigger biased thinking. When discussing one competency across several people, instead of one person at the time, it reduces unconsciously biased comparisons to a stereotype. The discussion is instead **anchored on the evidence** shared about the competency performance.

Additionally, using a designed template or checklist for the rating of the candidates against the pre-selected competencies (see the Inclusion Nudge **STRUCTURED SCORING OF 6 QUALIFICATIONS** (→ page 126)) helps to ensure that we stick to the agreed upon process, helps to reduce the influence of bias in interview notetaking, and helps to objectively frame up the interview panel discussion when making the decision on who to hire.

Inclusive Evaluations & Decisions

# Colour Code People to Ensure Meritocracy

## The Challenge

When people are promoting other people, they often think they are being objective. However, affinity bias (an unconscious pull towards people who are similar to ourselves) takes over. We tend to prefer people we know better than those we don't. This is further complicated by the influence of stereotypes more than merit as we evaluate other people. When **Stephen Frost**, the CEO of Frost Included, was working with a leadership group and they were rating talent for readiness for promotion, he noticed biased patterns. This is what he designed to address this challenge.

### The Inclusion Nudge

Colour code people when evaluating their performance and potential as part of a people calibration process.

Use a colour for various diversity metrics: man, woman, introvert, extrovert, ethnicity dominant in headquarters, minority ethnicity, long tenure, short tenure, and other.

Write the name of every candidate using the assigned colour and add to one of the three categories: 'ready now', 'ready in 1 year', and 'ready in 2 years'.

Identify patterns in colours and categories together.

**Purpose:** This helps leaders to see potential biased patterns, implicit norms, and stereotypes, such as 'men ready now', 'women ready in 2 years', and 'extroverts ready now', 'introverts ready in 2 years', and other patterns that may emerge.

|  Ready now  |  Ready in 1 Year  |  Ready in 2 Years  |
| --- | --- | --- |

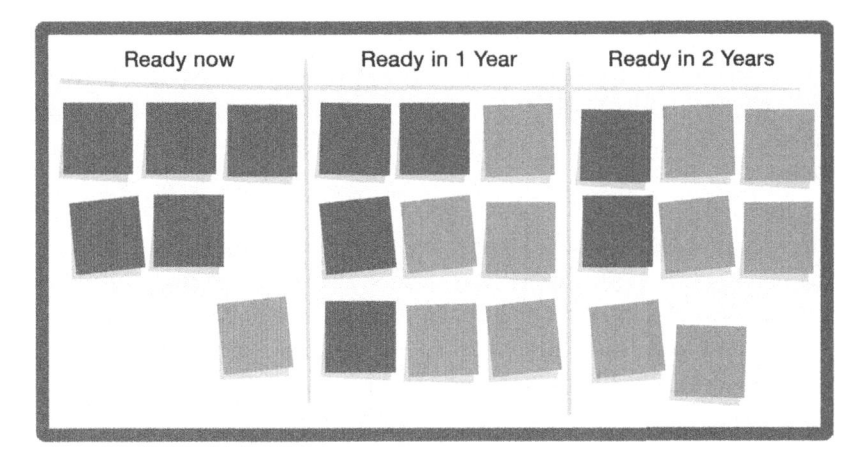

*Image created by Christina Hucke*

## How To

**1** Set up the room with three columns on a whiteboard, three flip charts, or three posters on the walls.

**2** Instruct the members of the promotion committee or leaders to place their candidates in the three buckets of 'ready now', 'ready in 1 year' and 'ready in 2 years'.

In the original version of this design, the committee members were invited to write their candidates on the whiteboard where men were written in blue and women in green. Blue is stereotypically male and green is associated with 'go' or 'proceed'. This can also be done by using coloured sticky notes.

**3** Identify the patterns based on the colours in the three categories.

**4** Then, attribute relevant data to the names, such as 360 feedback, performance review feedback, sales, KPIs, etc. to make a fact-based and merit-based evaluation.

**5** Talk about the difference and improved balance in men and women being ready now and in 1 or 2 years by applying facts.

## Impact

Stephen shares that when the committee saw the results, they were quite shocked because all the people in the 'ready now' category were blue (men) and most of the 'ready in 2 years' were green (women).

The impact was immediate in that promotion committee members could see the impact of their bias. There were women and some men in the 'ready in 2 years' category with better KPI's than those who were in the 'ready now' category. It was a visual representation of suboptimal decision making. Some people were shocked, some felt validated, and some were at first defensive, but it gave everyone a shared understanding of the problem. This then allowed the team to discuss why candidates were where they were and what they wanted to redesign in the process to increase meritocracy.

This process design also prompted some difficult conversations about affinity bias, objectivity, and the skills required. And it did lead to an increase in women being promoted over the three years that this process was applied. Some changes were immediate, such as with 'in the moment' re-evaluations of the promotion decisions. However, the major changes happened year 2 onwards when people knew what was coming and would take pre-emptive action, for example when realising that someone was objectively better and placing them in a different bucket.

Overall, this was a positive change, says Stephen. This process became the default and was accepted as a good check-and-balance design against bias and to improve the meritocracy of the decision-making process overall.

This design also removed the pressure from the diversity protagonist as a 'lobbyist' and moved them into a process of 'facilitator' where the leaders or committee members were debating amongst themselves rather than challenging the process of making the system more diverse and inclusive.

## Authors' Comments & Behavioural Insights

This can also function as a motivational intervention, what we call a *Feel the Need* Inclusion Nudge, if you need to ensure buy-in from from other leaders in your organisation to make this an integrated part of the evaluation and decision-making process about who to promote. Here's how to do that.

### Create a *Feel the Need* Inclusion Nudge to get buy-in

The participants in the evaluation process start by writing the names of their candidates on similar colour sticky notes and add those to the three categories. Then, ask them to write the names of their candidates again, but this time on different coloured sticky notes; one colour for men and one colour for women, and then add the names again to the three categories next to the others. Do it again for introvert and extrovert (or some other dimension such as nationality, age group, etc.) and add to the three categories next to the two other patterns. You might be in a situation or position where you don't have the power or mandate to ask this of the leaders. If this is the case, then you do it yourself by simply putting one colour sticky notes with the names of men and another colour with the names of women. Ask them *"What patterns do you notice?"*. In this way you can visualise several biases and patterns at the same time and this will be a major eye-opener for them and motivate for them to support implementing this process action.

Colour coding is a technique you can use in several of the steps in a talent selection process, as well as in other decision-making processes, such as idea pitching, idea generation, innovation projects, and much more. It's so simple, yet so powerful.

Inclusive Evaluations & Decisions

# Neutral Observer in Evaluation Meetings

## The Challenge

To help ensure a lessening of bias in talent discussions, designing the talent assessment discussions to include ways to capture bias in action and address it in the discussion can be powerful de-biasing process step. This can help to bring greater objectivity and fairer talent assessments for the organisation and the employees. This is how **Charlotte Sweeney** ✊🏾, the founder of Charlotte Sweeney Associates, has been working as a neutral observer in organisations' talent discussions.

> **The Inclusion Nudge**
>
> Use 'neutral' observation and feedback from the observer
> (plus a video recording)
> as an integrated part of the talent review process

**Purpose:** Capture and reveal when bias is occurring in talent discussions, and address in the meeting to ensure more objective assessments and selection of candidates.

## How To

Apply this nudge for more inclusive evaluations when it is relevant, such as during talent reviews, succession planning, and promotions period. Having a neutral observer as part of any evaluation discussion can add value, regardless of that being about research grants, peer reviews, innovation projects, funding, investment, film subsidies, or other situations.

## Securing the leaders support

### Prepare
Be sure to have the understanding and agreement from all participants to video record the meeting. If you use a neutral observer in an interview situation, do not use video when the candidate is there, but only in the interview committee's evaluation discussion afterwards.

### Discuss
At the start of the evaluation meeting, call out that the role of the neutral observer is purely to observe throughout. Share there will be questions from the observer after the discussion process finishes and a review of some of the footage.

### Debrief
Once the decisions on hiring or promotions have been made, ask the participants to reflect on these types of questions:

*"How easy was it to come to a consensus about who would be promoted?"*
*"Do you feel that you and the team have been fair and equitable throughout the process?"*
*"Were there any words and phrases used for the different candidates that you discussed?"*
*"Could any biases have slipped into your discussion?"*

Then, replay parts of the video for all in the room to see and hear the discussions and to also watch their body language on the screen. Continue the discussion about what was happening throughout the meeting after they watched some of the footage. Ask them to call out any patterns noticed and could these have impacted the promotion (or other topic) decisions made? Review the talent decisions again.

In the post-discussion debrief, before reviewing the video, Charlotte says that all felt they had given the candidates a fair review and that the right people were going to get promoted. None of the attendees could recall any examples where they had spoken about the promotions differently.

Charlotte then shared a couple of examples that she had observed, including:

*"You referred to one male as committed to his role, not ready for the promotion yet but at risk of leaving if you didn't promote him this year. You also spoke about a female candidate who you thought was 90 % ready this year but that an extra year would make sure she was **really** ready. What was the difference between those two decisions?"*

*"You referred to one person who was excelling at their job and had outstanding performance ratings for the last four years; however, you didn't know if you should promote this person because the new manager in that area has a 'thing' about people without a degree. How did that shape your thinking?"*

While there were a number of other examples that she shared to gain their views on their decision-making process, many couldn't recall those specific aspects of the discussions and were not sure they had actually been said. Although this process did take some time to complete, it was clear that many in the room had not consciously been aware of some of the comments or body language until they watched the video.

### Undercover observer to get support

Like many of us doing this work, sometimes we don't have strong support from the leaders or process owners to openly call out bias in talent discussions or elsewhere. An internal change maker who had been hired to address the low representation of diverse talents in leadership roles shared an example like this with us. Although the change maker had been given the mandate for change ('fix this'), key stakeholders were not included nor accountable for this change mandate. Her requests to several people for her to sit in the talent review meetings were 'politely' ignored or outrightly denied. Business and HR leaders were not willing for her to express questions about the influence of bias in the talent selection discussions and process. The success of the change mandate was at risk if she could not be even in the room where talent discussions and decisions were happening.

What this change maker did was to re-frame her request. The talent review meetings occurred during the first weeks that she was in the role. Having had rejection from her earlier requests to be a part of the talent discussions and call out where bias may be influencing (her mandate), she used another tactic in her next request to a different leader. Her request was re-framed to be part of her orientation to the organisation since she was new. She appealed to the leader helping her integrate into the company. With this re-framing and shift in the focal anchor to be on her rather than the leaders, she got support to sit in and observe the talent review meetings.

Over the many days of talent review discussions across all parts of the organisation, the change maker was a silent observer but was very active in taking notes. To others in the meeting, it seemed as if the change maker was taking notes on the talents in the organisation who were being discussed. At the end of the talent review cycle, she complied the pages and pages of notes taken of biased comments into theme clusters, supplemented with how frequently they occurred, and several actual quotes of what was said. In the next regular meeting with her manager (the CEO), she shared the overview with him. He read the report and reflected on his role in the talent discussions, and the outcomes of the talents who were discussed (both those who had favouritism bias that supported their career advancement and those who had negative bias that detracted on their career opportunities). The CEO then shared the findings with his executive leadership team.

### Online design version

This can be easily be done in online meetings. You simply follow the same instructions. The observer can report back in real time to the group verbally, or by the whiteboard, or by using the chat feature. The report back needs to be direct quotes (word by word) what was said. Or the observation can be done in two parts by using the recording feature in the online meeting platform. First conduct the discussion, then do the debrief by replaying for all the recording of the meeting and have a facilitated discussion that engages all to call out where biases may have cropped up in the talent review as described in the how to steps. This can actually have an even stronger impact than just saying it to people because 'seeing is believing'.

## Impact

Charlotte explains that it only takes a few minutes for all attendees to feel comfortable and forget about the recording. After watching the playback of the video, they felt they needed to review some of the decisions and discuss again. Different decisions were made in a few cases. Feedback from the attendees was hugely positive. They felt more aware of the impact unconscious bias had on their everyday decision making. As a result of the exercise, the process of recording the discussions and reviewing the videos as a decision-making team was introduced throughout the promotions process for a specific region and recommended for delivery in other regions.

In the case of the (anonymous) internal change maker, the observation report and the subsequent discussion made the CEO and leaders *feel the need* for a change. It led to the change maker gaining the support needed to change the talent review process to call out bias in the moment through the use of a neutral observer in the discussions. It also shifted the change mandate to not be only 'hers' but that of decision makers (leaders) and talent process owners.

## Authors' Comments & Behavioural Insights

Having a change mandate and showing some leaders and evaluators the data, imbalances, and biases might still not be enough to motivate them to support the suggestion to invite an observer to be part of the selection process. The data might not be enough for them to see the problem. The thought of being observed might trigger feeling of discomfort, insecurity, or fear, and lead to a rejection of the suggestion. To avoid this and ensure support for the observer intervention, make sure you design some *Feel the Need* Inclusion Nudges. You can learn more about how you can do this in the *Action Guide for Motivating Allies*.

### Why it works: behavioural insights
This Inclsuion Nudge is powerful if you can get an organisation to agree to have their talent management discussions recorded and make it an integrated part of the process design when discussing talent. Here are some of the behavioural insights explaining why this works.

**Being seen**
The observation itself can have an equally important impact as the feedback afterwards. The fact that the leaders and evaluators know they are being **'seen'** is very likely in itself to change their behaviour, meaning that it's not solely by watching the recording the change happens. Research has shown how individuals modify their behaviour when under observation (being 'studied' and 'singled' out),[120] and another study showed how pictures of eyes

on a piece of paper increased ethics and moral behaviour.[121] The pictures of eyes functioned as **salient cues that prime** the unconscious mind and fostered specific behaviour.

**Seeing is believing**
The recording of the discussions is also a *Feel the Need* Inclusion Nudge, when the leaders and evaluators watch it afterwards. This is because it holds a mirror to the leader's own spoken and non-verbal communications regarding talent to reflect upon what is often unreflected. This can motivate change because seeing their own behaviour on video, shifts awareness and seeing is believing.[122] That's how the unconscious mind works. It's much better to *show* than *tell*, if you want change because it motivates the unconscious mind which is the system doing our behaviour.

**Seeing the gap**
Asking reflective questions and afterwards showing the recording are impactful because the leaders and evaluators can see the gap themselves. By first asking them about their own perception of their fairness in the process, most will answer in accordance with their self-perception more than based on how fair they acted in the process. The gap is realised by then afterwards showing them the facts about their actual (biased) behaviour. Seeing this gap can in itself help alter behaviour in the long-term and not just in this session.[123]

## Inclusive Evaluations & Decisions

# Put on the Gender Lens When Evaluating

## The Challenge

While the common perception is that women advance up the corporate ladder until they reach a "glass ceiling", the reality is different. Women actually drop off at almost every level. Changing this requires understanding what is going on. Mostly, it is due to unconscious biases from both women and men, as well as the corporate cultures and norms that influence how talent is perceived. Unconscious bias and organisational norms have a strong impact on our perceptions and evaluations of people in, for example, performance reviews. Attention will be paid to different kinds of information depending on whether the employee is female or male. Hence, different performance standards may unintentionally be applied to women and men. The challenge is how to make the evaluations gender neutral. **Anita Cassagne**, the Head of Leadership and Inclusion at Nestlé France, shared an intervention that she designed in her former role with Nestlé Waters to change this in the evaluation of talents.

### The Inclusion Nudge

In the second round of evaluations,
put on a pair of paper "glasses" as a prompter to
"Put on your gender lens"
in reviewing the initial evaluation of performance.

**Purpose:** Use a physical prompter to change the perception of what is seen and how evaluations are done, by keeping attention on how gender bias influences the evaluation and discussion.

## How To

This was designed for the people calibration process in a private company, but it's applicable in all evaluations of people, performance, ideas, potential, and much more.

**❶** The paper glasses come with a brochure with specific actions to take to apply a gender lens.

**❷** Design the material/brochure with information and enablers on how to mitigate bias and with the paper glasses. The material is on the table during a talent discussion and used to qualify the evaluation process.

**❸** Discuss each candidate.

**❹** When all candidates have been discussed, dedicate part of the discussion to women in the talent pipeline. Ask the leaders as part of this process step to read the brochure and put on the 'gender glasses'. Talk about performance, potential, competencies, and skills, using supporting evidence to illustrate situations to make sure all potential gender biases are eliminated. Instruct participants to not talk about the employee's personal situation.

**5** If high-potential women are removed from the list, the manager should account for the removal. Challenge assumptions. You can use the *Process Design* Inclusion Nudge **'IF NOT, WHY NOT' ACCOUNTABILITY** (→ page 71) for inspiration.

**6** Implement supporting actions, such as create clear career development plans step by step for all high-potential women and follow up on the implementation. Support their development and track their career and progress. And review job assignments of top talents on an annual basis to ensure they are working on projects with high visibility, developmental opportunities, and impact.

## Impact

Anita shared that this forced a shift in the discussion in the evaluation process. It kept attention on lessening gender bias in the discussions and it held each other accountable. This resulted in having a more qualified and gender-neutral performance discussion.

## Authors' Comments & Behavioural Insights

The 'gender glasses' is a playful and powerful way to illustrate the importance of the 'lens' we see with. The physical symbol calls for a pause in the process to reflect on how the previous talent discussion went relative to the stated intentions of evaluating performance based on merit and working towards gender balance. Symbols are often more powerful than words, and deeply embedded in the subconscious and processed rapidly. The 'gender glasses' triggered the needed action for 're-looking' by putting on the glasses after the first round of talent discussions, triggering a review of the discussion and the results.

Many Inclusion Nudges have more impact when combined with other Inclusion Nudges. This *Framing Perceptions* Inclusion Nudge could be combined with the *Process Design* Inclusion Nudge on changing the default from *'Who is ready?'* to *'All are ready now'*: **DEFAULT AS 'ALL QUALIFIED' & 'WHY NOT'** (→ page 138).

## Why it works: behavioural insights
### Perspective taking

This is an active cognitive process of imagining the world from another vantage point. **Perspective taking** has repeatedly been found to decrease prejudice and stereotyping. Perspective taking has also been shown to help people create value and maximise benefits by adding issues that weren't initially considered. Evidence also suggests that consciously focusing on perspective taking can make teams more effective and more creative and can prompt people into deeper, more complex thinking that results in better outcomes. You can read more about this in a summary of this research by Gillian Ku, who is an Associate Professor of Organisational Behaviour at London Business School.[124]

Changing perspectives can also happen with *role assignment and questions*, that **primes a new perspective,** like one leadership group did when they were in trouble. They asked: *"If we get kicked out and the board brought in a new leadership team, what do you think they would do?"*. This example is referenced in the book *Wiser* by Sunstein and Hastie.[125]

### Props

We can find help to change perspectives in **'props'** that can make us **'see-feel-change',**[126] such as *physical objects* like the paper 'gender glasses' used in this Inclusion Nudge from Anita. The Heath brothers also illustrate the power of this with a real-life example in their book *Switch* where 429 work gloves were collected and put on a table to get the leadership team to see the current procurement process in a **new perspective.**[127]

### Technology solutions

Today, virtual reality (VR) has taken **perspective taking** to new levels by allowing people using VR glasses to go beyond imagining the perspective of other people by merging the self with 'the other'. More and more organisations, companies, and NGO's are using VR technology to foster empathy, reduce bias, reduce domestic violence against women, enable people with autism, and more. The United Nations is using VR interventions designed to help viewers see the perspective of the humanitarian refugee crisis from a human perspective, emphatise with refugees, and to catalyse change.[128]

Similarly, the paper glasses in this *Framing Perspectives* Inclusion Nudge example can apply a new 'perspective' to the situation.

Inclusive Evaluations & Decisions

# Difference as Criterion for Selection, Not De-Selection

## The Challenge

There is a well-known unconscious bias called the "mini-me" that can influence recruitment decisions, whereby we tend to prefer candidates similar to ourselves. This bias can prevent selecting the best candidates and benefiting from the recruitment of a diverse mix of thinking styles, capabilities, and life experiences. This is how **Janina Norton**, Head of Employee Engagement at AXA Investment Managers helped hiring managers change their perception on candidates and diversity and is inspiration on how leaders can do this with their fellow leaders as well.

### The Inclusion Nudge

As an integrated part of the selection of candidates at the beginning of the recruitment process, have recruiters ask the hiring manager questions to prod 'difference' as a selection criterion.

The recruiter asks the hiring manager questions as on the next page.

After the interview, check for patterns in 'differences' among candidate, manager, and team.

> "What attributes or traits do you not have, that it would be ideal for the new candidate to have?"
>
> "How could this candidate's detail-orientation style supplement your [the manager] big-picture orientation?"
>
> "What traits would be useful for the candidate to have that don't 'fit' with the current team, which might mix things up and create more diverse perspectives?"

**Purpose:** Demote preferences for similarity in the evaluation and decision-making process by reframing the perception of difference from being a burden to being a resource, and thus promote behaviours that support that happening.

## How To

Ideally, all leaders, recruiters and hiring managers within an organisation should have some understanding on the impact unconscious bias on decisions during recruitment.

❶ Before advertising, the hiring manager and recruiter meet to discuss the approach that will be taken to recruit. There is usually already a formal set of questions for this conversation, to discuss what attributes, skills, and experience the ideal candidate will have. An additional area of questioning is added to this briefing questionnaire. These questions frame 'difference' as an asset for the team, manager, and purpose.

❷ After the interview, check for patterns in differences among candidates, the manager, and the current team. Revisit the original briefing document. Raise questions and discuss whether the selected candidate has different traits than the team currently has which would benefit the team and the work.

❸ Refer to specific difference identified as valuable by the hiring manager: *"Does this new candidate deliver a different style of working, a different set of life experiences, or a way of thinking that is currently missing within the team?"*. It makes the individual candidate's differences a conscious criteria for selection, rather than the unconscious criteria for de-selection.

## Impact

Adding this process change at the stage before short-listing and interviewing provides an opportunity for the hiring manager to reflect on how a different perspective or life experience could benefit the team. This helps managers challenge themselves to identify these differences and realise the value of diverse attributes.

It also provides an **anchor** for supporting the hiring manager to make the selection decision.

## Authors' Comments & Behavioural Insights

We recommend to further strengthen this action, that you make the patterns of 'de-selection' arguments and 'selection' arguments from previous recruitment processes visible. Do this using a pre-designed template or list. Managers make marks on the template to ensure that their own patterns are visible. View and discuss possible implications of the patterns.

The reason this is important to do, is because it **reduces complexity** and helps to **see the hidden patterns.** Both of these are key design elements in reducing the impact of bias in talent selection decisions.

Inclusive Evaluations & Decisions

# List Pros & Cons to Counter Biased Evaluations

## The Challenge

As described in previous Inclusion Nudge examples, a large body of research shows that bias influences the evaluations of men and women. Women are more likely to be judged harder. Women have to be better qualified to be viewed as competent as a man, and they are also viewed harder in terms of their personality. Women get more negative reviews of their personality (they are *"too assertive"*, or *"too soft"*, or *"not enough charismatic"*, or *"too close to their team"*, or *"too emotional"*, or *"not collaborative enough"*, etc.). Whereas men are reviewed more on their future potential to improve on their qualifications rather than based on their past performance.[129] As one researcher summed up, *"Because of gender bias and the way in which it influences evaluation in work settings, being competent provides no assurance that a woman will advance to the same organisational levels as an equivalently performing man."*[130]

**Tinna C. Nielsen,** Founder of Move the Elephant for Inclusiveness, and **Lisa Kepinski,** Founder of Inclusion Institute, have worked with many organisations to help mitigate bias in their processes. Here is a simple but effective technique that they have offered to organisations to help spot when bias may have been present in their talent evaluations.

## The Inclusion Nudge

List the pro (positive) and con (negative) arguments in a template and divide the candidates by gender. Look for patterns in pro and con arguments across gender.

**Purpose:** See patterns of gender bias in terms of negative and positive comments about the candidates.

## How To

This process design is as simple as described above. Develop a template before the evaluation and selection process to ensure consistency. This will require less effort of the evaluators to do (and thus, more likelihood that it will be done and done objectively). On this template have these sections.

### ❶ Pre-commitment statement

Have a space at the top of the template for each evaluator to write their process pre-commitment statement and sign their name beneath it.

An example of a pre-commitment statement is

*"I want to make fair and objective decisions, and by looking from multiple perspectives, I can be more equitable and a better leader in evaluations."*

You can make this even stronger by having a photo of the person or a photo of the full evaluation team next to this statement.

Each person should then read aloud to the group or to a person next to them, their pre-commitment statement.

## ❷ Pros & cons list
→ Have the form divided in half with pros on one side and cons on the other.
→ List your arguments and facts and share with others on the evaluation team.
→ Invite each other to critique the listing to avoid confirmation bias and overconfidence bias that may be steering responses to align with their previous decision.

## ❸ Reflection, data gathering, & pattern spotting
Include some additional prompting reflection questions, such as

*"If she was a he, then would I have said the same thing?"*
*"What would we lose if we don't go with this person?"*
*"What emotions does this person trigger for me?"*
*"Who do I think about when I consider this person?"*

Add in some further review analysis action steps, such as

*"What are the words and phrases that have been used about this person?"*

Write these down, and then ask

*"What patterns do I see?"*
*"Is the reference point the same for all being evaluated?"*
*"Did we use past performance or future potential? If both, then were they equally discussed? Are there any patterns?"*

Also, examine for equity in using the same frame of reference for the assessment; identify if it was based on past (performance) and/or future (projection of potential).

## ❹ Decision making
Use the list to help inform the evaluation decision. Review to see if there are any missing information or open questions. Also, the team may want to use a collective ranking of the reasons put forth for and against. With all the data insights shared, the group can be in a stronger position to make the decision.

## Impact

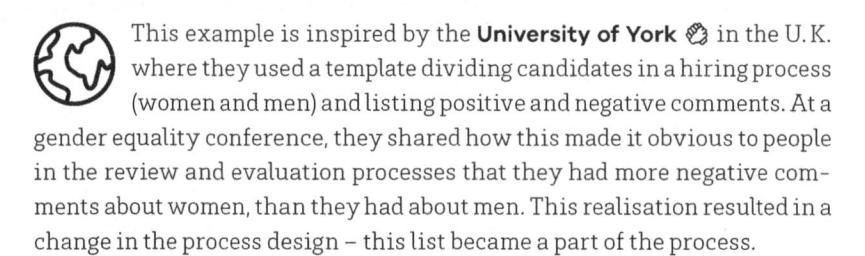

This example is inspired by the **University of York** 🌍 in the U.K. where they used a template dividing candidates in a hiring process (women and men) and listing positive and negative comments. At a gender equality conference, they shared how this made it obvious to people in the review and evaluation processes that they had more negative comments about women, than they had about men. This realisation resulted in a change in the process design – this list became a part of the process.

At a film institute where **Tinna Nielsen** worked, they designed a template to help film commissioners spot potential biased patterns of pro and con arguments, as well as positive and negative comments about film-funding applicants. Those who used the template when evaluating and reviewing the quality of film scripts and applications, reported that it made a significant difference. They could see patterns that had an influence on the final outcome. This gave them opportunities to reflect and improve the reviewing.

## Authors' Comments & Behavioural Insights

This kind of list can be used in several situations – it could be when evaluating ideas for investments, awarding research grants, films for funding, applicants for jobs, people for projects, students for schools. Think about it – there are so many situations where this could be relevant.

The process design example given here is based on gender stereotypes biasing the evaluation process. However, it can be adapted for any other social group stereotypes, such as nationality, age group, etc.

This should be ideally done as a built-in, automatic part of the process of evaluations. However, you may need to get others onboard with doing this as a first step. This was the case with some organisations that **Lisa Kepinski**, Founder of Inclusion Institute, worked with. As a first step, they did a retrospective review over past talent evaluations (a randomly-selected sample) to reveal how different language, frames of reference, amount of words used, and ratings showed up by gender, length of service, nationality, and job function. With this, she designed a *Feel the Need* Inclusion Nudge to show the challenge based on the leaders' own perceptions of what they thought was the case (fair evaluations) and what the data actually revealed (inequity).

From this 'aha' experience, the leaders supported designing ways to catch biased evaluations **during** the process and before it was finalised (such as before the evaluation rating was approved within the system by inviting others to review for the influence of bias, and they did this for other colleagues).

### Why it works: behavioural insights

**Simplicity** aids the likelihood that this de-biasing intervention will be done. It can even be done on the spot (assuming already familiar with the design) with no pre-created template, but just with something to write with and write on.

**Slowing down** our decision making is a good way to reduce the risk of system 1 automatic thinking and the reliance on stereotypes and other biases. The time and thinking that it takes to complete the pros & cons list and analysis, helps to activate system 2 cognitive functioning, and thus ensures better control (slow vs fast thinking) on the decision-making process.

The listing of the arguments for and against an evaluation decision also helps to **break down the complexity** of the task and reduce the **cognitive overload** in decision making. Heavy mental effort by too much information, ambiguity, and time pressure for a decision are conditions for biases to occur.

Also, it helps to activate **self-distance**, or **perspective taking**, in the decision-making process. When our rationales and arguments are more visible to us and others involved, then the greater the objectivity (the **eyes on us effect**).

You can combine this Inclusion Nudge with another *Process Design* **STRUCTURED SCORING OF 6 QUALIFICATIONS** (→ page 126 in this Action Guide).

Inclusive Evaluations & Decisions

# Write Your Feedback Before Reading Others

## The Challenge

During the interview process, candidate evaluations can often be accessed by all members on the interview committee. The challenge is that a typical interview process includes several interviewers, who each assess a different core competency such as collaboration or customer focus when meeting with a candidate. **Chuck Edward**, the Corporate Vice President for Global Talent Acquisition at Microsoft, explains that in their interview process, each interviewer would enter their evaluation and feedback into a portal, with this feedback visible to the entire interview team at any time. This setup had the potential for one interviewer to read others' comments and hiring recommendations before meeting with the candidate. By learning of other people's perception of a candidate, it could influence how an interviewer thinks about them the potentially bias their assessment. This is how Microsoft decided to change the default and the order of actions.

### The Inclusion Nudge

Shift the default in the hiring tool to: 'write first, then read'.

Change the IT system that captures interview evaluations and feedback, such that each interviewer on an interview team is prompted to immediately write and enter their own evaluation of the candidate, before being able to read the evaluation and feedback of the others.

**Purpose:** Ensure interviewers provide feedback without being influenced by what others think to help reduce any influence of bias and for more objective feedback, which has been proven to produce a more inclusive and diverse hiring culture. Unbiased assessment isn't possible if interviewers know what others think.

## How To

Microsoft changed their tool that captures interview feedback, such that interviewers at an event or on an interview loop are prompted to immediately enter their own opinion about the candidate *before* being able to see others' comments. Here is how they did this.

The interview feedback portal was adjusted such that only after an interviewer submits their feedback, are they able to view what others have provided. Once feedback has been submitted, the interviewer is unable to edit their comments, thus preventing an interviewer from changing their mind based on feedback from other interviewers.

The intention behind this shift is not to limit access to feedback, but to change the timing of when people see what others' have entered. With the default: **Write first, then read,** there are no restrictions on sharing that feedback, once submitted. The feedback is not private. An interviewer can see all others' feedback once they've submitted their own.

Beyond the update to the interview feedback technology, they implemented several change management strategies, as described below.

### ❶ Explain the why
The foundation of their change management strategy was explaining the rationale behind the move to objective feedback. Their readiness materials were explicit in describing the research on bias, and alignment of this change with Microsoft's commitment to creating an inclusive hiring culture.

### ❷ Be prescriptive and specific in the feedback process
Best practice is to set aside 10-15 minutes after the interview to capture your interview feedback. This allows the interviewers to enter the informa-

tion while it's still fresh in their mind and provides the hiring manager and recruiter with a current view of the interview process. There may be competencies or subject areas that the interviewer had hoped to discuss with a candidate, or topics that they wanted to discuss in more detail. It's appropriate for the interviewer to contact upcoming interviewers and provide that guidance without disclosing their assessment of the candidate.

**Provide examples of how interviewers should and should not coordinate or share information outside the feedback tool.**

An appropriate example is

*"It would be great if you could dig in on ... (call out a specific core competency, such as, ... Influencing for Impact ... we should hear more about times when the candidate needed to persuade someone to complete a task without any authority over that person."*

An inappropriate example is

*"It would be great if you could dig in on ..." (call out a specific core competency, such as, "... Influencing for Impact – the candidate seemed weak in that area and I'm not sure they could handle a role where they needed to get others outside their team to complete work."*

! Do not create "workarounds" to share candidate assessment information using email, work collaboration sites, messaging tools, etc. Frame this as *"We run significant risk to the company by keeping this information outside our recruiting systems, in violation of General Data Protection Regulation (GDPR) guidelines."*

## Impact

This Inclusion Nudge was recently (2019) implemented at Microsoft, and they look forward to collating feedback and reviewing the results over time. Yet, they're confident in this move. Their decision to move to objective feedback was data- and research-backed. They know that people are impressionable. When we are exposed to other's opinions before forming our own, we tend to anchor on the existing view.[131]

More generally, the 'wisdom of the crowd' depends on the independence of the respective opinions within the crowd.[132] Yet, that independence is easily compromised, in many ways—anchoring, of course, but also common backgrounds, training, friends, etc. As Chuck shares in this example, you may think you're getting 5 to 6 opinions when effectively you're getting only 1.5![133]

In Chuck's work at Microsoft, they have designed a hiring process that explicitly pushes against these compromising factors. The first is don't let people talk to each other or see other's opinions before providing their own, which this Inclusion Nudge example addresses. Additionally, expose the candidate to judges in different ways and at different points in time, and also, bring people with different perspectives into the process.

## Authors' Comments & Behavioural Insights

In Microsoft they redesigned the IT portal, but you can also apply this process design when you don't use an online tool. Make sure people make up their mind and write their view, before getting access to the views of others.

To address the other aspects that Chuck offered in this example of what makes a good hiring process, look at other *Process Design* Inclusion Nudges, such as **JOB INTERIVEW IN TWO PARTS** (→ page 198), and consider developing a checklist as in the Inclusion Nudge example **STRUCTURED SCORING OF 6 QUALIFICATIONS** (→ page 126) to support having a diverse interview panel rather than relying on good will.

### Why it works: behavioural insights
There are several biases that can be activated when we hear the views of others prior to having our own experience in interviews and other evaluation discussions. Some of these are listed below and they are primarily unconscious patterns, but may also operate consciously, as well.

**Priming bias:** steering our thinking, judgement and beaviour towards what is suggested, or 'primed'

**Confirmation bias:** only seeking out and acknowledging information that proves an already held perspective, and overlooking negating evidence

**Self-silencing:** holding back on voicing your views due to cognitive and social dynamics, such as power imbalances, status, perceived expertise in others, social risk and other negative consequences for voicing your perspective, exclusion from the group, etc.

**Group conformity:** going along with, even may voice agreement with, a view put forth by others which the group endorses, or by the majority in the group, even when you may hold some doubt about it

These biases can reinforce each other and deepen the impact of bias within the team's talent selection process. Bias is actually amplified in groups and mistakes can result.[134] To make the best decisions, we need to design ways to reduce the impact of these mental errors. We need to ensure that our processes and tools enable objectivity.

> **WHAT & HOW**
> I'll make sure to be inclusive in evaluations & decisions

Inclusive Interviewing

# Interview Bundles to Bust Bias

## The Challenge

**?** When people interview one-to-one, they think they are being objective in the interview situation, evaluation, and selection, but they are unfortunately usually biased. At the London Organising Committee of the Olympic Games 2012, **Stephen Frost**, CEO of Frost Included and former Head of Diversity & Inclusion at the London Organising Committee of the Olympic and Paralympic Games, implemented two interventions to reduce bias. One was to have interview panels of a minimum of three people in order to have as many diverse perspectives and behaviours available. The other intervention was the one described below.

> ### The Inclusion Nudge
>
> Interview candidates in groups of 5-8 people.

**Purpose:** Reduce stereotypes and biases and force the unconscious mind to focus on performance and avoid unconscious comparison to a stereotype or homogeneous patterns.

## How To

Make sure to have a strategic workforce plan in place so you know what talent you actually want and what gaps currently exist in your staff.

Identify, based on the workforce plan, the positions that you need people for and what skills you need for those positions. This will become the hiring competency criteria. Use this intervention of group interview with more generic positions and when you are hiring for multiple openings/positions of the same kind of role, for example 5 programme managers.

For positions where you need to hire 5 people, then shortlist 15, and interview in 3 groups of 5 and choose 2 candidates per group, or interview 8 and choose 4 candidates. The larger the group, the more powerful the diversity nudge.

The interview panel should have a mix of gender and functions.

Give the candidates an exercise/task to solve that is related to the job for which you are hiring. The candidates are solving the task in the room as a group. There are no specific framing instructions other than solve the task to the best of your ability.

The interview panel evaluates the candidates, such as in an assessment centre, by observing their behaviour and skills accordingly to the predetermined qualification criteria. Group the candidates all together but with each person assessed individually based on the group exercise.

Do two rounds of interviews. In the 1st interview, the hiring manager participates as part of the interview panel. In the 2nd interview, the hiring manager is not participating to reduce any potential for bias.

Each interviewer scores the candidates on screening criteria independently. The interview panel compares scores only afterwards.

## Impact

The Olympic Games in London 2012 had the most diverse workforce in its history. Other inclusive practices were implemented in addition to the group interviews. The numbers speak for themselves and so do the stories.

Here are some impact examples on the workforce composition that Stephen shares.

→ Race: 60% White/40% Black, Asian, or minority ethnic
→ Gender/gender identity: 54% male/46% female (trans staff included)
→ Disability: 9% (deaf, disabled, or having a long-term health condition)
→ Sexual orientation: 5% declared lesbian, gay or bisexual
→ Age: 36% under 30, 15% over 50 with ranges from 16-79
→ Faith: All major faiths represented
→ Economic Inclusion/Social Mobility: 36% of hired people were previously unemployed and 23% came from the poorest boroughs in East London

A straight, White male, who was a venue manager, shared his experience with Stephen, saying that he *'would never have met people like that'* in his previous or next intended professional setting. He wouldn't have talked to *'them'* in the street or a bar, let alone work with them. They weren't *'his kind of people'* but they became his beloved team.

Furthermore, group interviews reduced cost and saved time. Also, in the situation of pressure to reduce the time to hire, this is a positive impact on what is usually is an anti-diversity process.

## Authors' Comments & Behavioural Insights

### Why it works: behavioural insights

As the research by Harvard Professor and Inclusion Nudge contributor Iris Bohnet has identified, this reduces stereotypes and biases and forces the unconscious mind to focus on performance. Also, we tend to select more variety in bundles. Research has revealed a pattern of choice characterized as a diversification bias. An experiment about choosing snacks for consumption illustrated how this works. People where asked to choose three snacks for eating for the next three days (one for each day) or choose one snack each day to eat on that day. Making the bundle choice of three snack made people pick three different snacks, while deciding on similar snacks when picking one each day. If people make combined choices they choose more variety. When interviewing in bundles we tend to select people representing more diversity.[113]

When people are evaluated in groups relative to each other, then their individual characteristics, such as gender, are **less salient.** Instead, their skill sets and how they interact with the group are more evident. In group interviews, the interviewers can see skills and attributes play out in real time.

Both of these Inclusion Nudge examples (Iris' one on joint evaluations, and this one from Stephen on group interviews) are based on **reference dependence** which is part of prospect theory and behavioural economics. As we make decisions, our automatic thinking employs a process of assessing the end results based on certain reference points and weighs these up against potential gains and losses. We are more inclined to avoid losses and risks, preferring to stay with what is known and comfortable. This can mean that we seek out people who remind us of the organisational norms, which are the reference points in the decision-making process. This maintains the status quo. Even when we may say we want more diversity our unconscious thinking can lead us askew from this. Designs such as joint evaluations, group interviews, and other examples of Inclusion Nudges help us to mitigate human decision-making biases.

We see more and more organisations using this process as part of their evaluation and selection process for their graduate and talent programmes. In addition to group interviews, candidates can also make group assignments and presentations.

Inclusive Interviewing

# The No CV Interview

## The Challenge

**?** As noted in other Inclusion Nudge examples, bias can arise during the candidate screening process when deciding who to select to progress further in the hiring process. We can be unduly influenced by the resume or application, including by seeing things like the candidates' identity information (name, photo, gender, nationality, race/ethnicity, age, etc.), the layout of the resume (amount of information, font, style, etc.), previous employers (activating the halo/horns effect by our admiration or dislike), similarities to the hiring evaluator (similar school, career path, where they live, hobbies, etc.), and more. There are several ways to address the unintended influence of bias.

We were inspired by an intervention that we read about which was designed to de-bias the screening and interview process at Cockroach Labs. In their blog on January 2017, **Lindsay Grenawalt** 🧠, their Chief People Officer, shared the approach they have implemented in this software company.

> **The Inclusion Nudge**
>
> Remove resumes from the interview process.

**Purpose:** Mitigate bias to hire the best qualified candidate.

## How To

This works with the recruiter still having access to the cv submitted by the applicant for the first screening step in the hiring process. If the decision is to proceed, then the resume is removed, as are any pre-screen notes.

Lindsay further shared that they learned it's important *"to prepare the candidate for this type of experience. … Prepping the candidate that the focus of the interview is on skills required for the job, helps prepare them for this. Without a resume, we only ask candidates about work, not their history."*[114]

## Impact

**Dave Delaney**, a recruiter at Cockroach Labs, says that they *"have found that once interviewers and candidates alike get past that initial shock and actually see the experience in action, it's generally well-received. For interviewers, they can focus entirely on the question(s) posed to the candidate, judging them purely on performance as opposed to having it skewed by details like the candidate's current company or academic background. Similarly, candidates can be confident that they are being assessed on their abilities rather than a sheet of paper."*[115] This approach *"resulted in more confident hiring decision"*.[116]

## Authors' Comments & Behavioural Insights

The reason why limiting the information we have about people is so important in talent selection is due to how our memory works. Our actions are **primed** by information and events of which we are not even aware. This happens even with really bizarre things.

### Why it works: behavioural insights

In an experiment, students (18-22 years old) were instructed to assemble four-word sentences from a set of five words. The group that had words associated with elderly, such as forgetful, bald, gray, or wrinkle, walked significantly slower when asked to walk to another room after the experiment than the group of student who had random (neutral) words. This is due to two kinds of priming; the set of words primed thoughts of old age, without mentioning the word 'old'; these thoughts primed a behaviour of walking slowly, which is associated with old age. All the students insisted that nothing they did after doing the scrambled sentences could have been influenced by the words they had worked with. This **priming** effect of the idea (of old age) influencing the action (walking slowly) is known as the **ideomotor effect**.[117]

This effect is also present in talent selection. Let's not rely on our own self-belief that we can control this. As bizarre as this might sound, it more bizarre to believe this does not influence you. Not seeing the CV is the kind of design needed to mitigate this kind of unconscious influence.

**Inclusive Interviewing**

# Participate in Interview by Phone

## The Challenge

Our assessment and selection decisions can be influenced by bias when we see candidates and this interferes with objectivity and decision making. Something as simple as the style or choice of clothing can influence the outcome. **Tinna C. Nielsen**, the Founder of Move the Elephant for Inclusiveness, shares this design that was used in an organisation where she previously worked.

> ### The Inclusion Nudge
>
> One member of the interview team participates in the job interviews by phone or online communication platform without video.

**Purpose:** Remove any impact of visual aspects from talent selection decisions to better focus on the person and their qualifications.

## How To

Members of the interview panel participate in the interviews in a different location. In Tinna's former job, the HR recruiters and the HR Business Partners often participated in the job interviews by phone because they were working in another location or country than where the interviews were physically taking place. This can also be done using video online communication platforms, but do it without video (audio only).

## Impact

This turned out to have an important influence on the evaluation of the candidates and decision-making process, because they could not be **influenced by the candidates' appearance.** They realised this because they noticed a pattern. When the interview committee was evaluating the candidates after the interviews, the recruiters on the phone always evaluated the candidates differently than the interviewers who were in the room and had met with the candidate in person. Then, one day, a recruiter asked *"What was the candidate wearing?"*.

The remote recruiters made it a part of the evaluation process, when this pattern would emerge, to always ask *"What was the candidate wearing?"* or *"How did the candidate look?"*.

It turned out that these questions were critical, because the majority of times, these **visual cues** had triggered bias. In one incident, the response was *"He was wearing jeans and a scarf!"* and then a judgement followed, *"That's an obvious sign that he does not understand the importance of dressing up and representing our company!"*. The remote recruiter replied, *"Or it's a sign that he had really made an effort to understand our company and our corporate identity and brand, because on our website we brand ourselves as a company and workplace that's casual, meeting our customers at 'eye level' and as a place where you can be who you are."*

This would then result in a constructive conversation, and a realisation that judging based on clothing is not a professional way to evaluate qualifications for a job, and they would reevaluate the merits.

This intervention is not only relevant in a hiring process, but also in investment pitching situations where **appearance, likability, and attractiveness** have been proven to have a significant impact.

Inclusive Interviewing

# Blind Interviews

## The Challenge

Through nine years of working with people who are blind and teaching them photography, it became clear to **Gina Badenoch**, Founder of Ojos que Sienten (a charity teaching blind people to do photography) and Capaxia consultancy, that many sighted people suffer from 'mental blindness' created by their own prejudices and stereotypes. We label people, objects, and situations very quickly using visual cues. Think of times when you have talked to someone without seeing them and later on saw them for the first time ... what shifted in your view of them? Could we actually make better decisions about people *without* seeing them?

> **The Inclusion Nudge**
>
> Blind job interviews.
> The interviewer(s) cannot see the candidate(s)
> in the beginning of the interview.

**Purpose:** Remove any impact of visual aspects from talent selection decisions to better focus on the person and their qualifications.

## How To

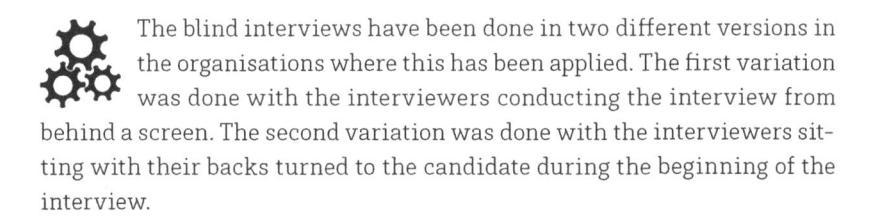

The blind interviews have been done in two different versions in the organisations where this has been applied. The first variation was done with the interviewers conducting the interview from behind a screen. The second variation was done with the interviewers sitting with their backs turned to the candidate during the beginning of the interview.

Next time you have the opportunity to interview somebody for a job at your organisation, try receiving them with your chair turned in the opposite direction to the candidate. Then, carry out the first five minutes of the interview without seeing them. This will no doubt be uncomfortable. However, it creates an opportunity to listen to the person and to form opinions without prejudging them from visual cues.

### Back-to-back

> Consider having both the candidates and the interviewers sit with their backs to each other. It could feel like social rejection to sit facing and talking to someone's back and this could unintentionally impact the candidates' full communication and performance.

Make sure to prepare the candidates by letting them know in advance that when they walk into the room there will be people (more than one to balance the bias each person may have and make sure to have a diverse group of interviewers) sitting with their backs toward the entrance or sitting behind a screen. Tell the candidates that the purpose is to help outsmart our unconscious bias and to heighten the interview discussion by really focusing on what is said rather than by visual cues.

After the first five minutes of the blind interview, ask the candidate if there's anything they would like to say before moving forward with the rest of the interview. At the end of the interview, ask for the candidates' comments from the experience. Also, get the comments from the interviewer team.

## Impact

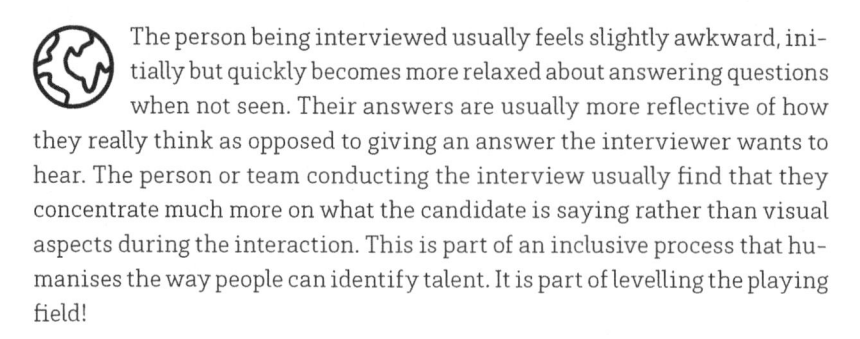

The person being interviewed usually feels slightly awkward, initially but quickly becomes more relaxed about answering questions when not seen. Their answers are usually more reflective of how they really think as opposed to giving an answer the interviewer wants to hear. The person or team conducting the interview usually find that they concentrate much more on what the candidate is saying rather than visual aspects during the interaction. This is part of an inclusive process that humanises the way people can identify talent. It is part of levelling the playing field!

## Authors' Comments & Behavioural Insights

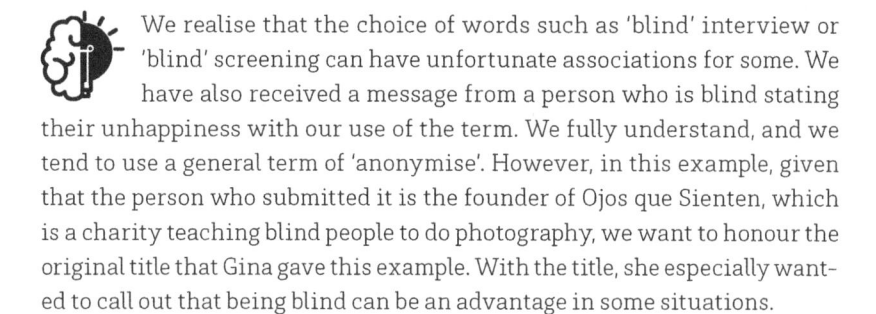

We realise that the choice of words such as 'blind' interview or 'blind' screening can have unfortunate associations for some. We have also received a message from a person who is blind stating their unhappiness with our use of the term. We fully understand, and we tend to use a general term of 'anonymise'. However, in this example, given that the person who submitted it is the founder of Ojos que Sienten, which is a charity teaching blind people to do photography, we want to honour the original title that Gina gave this example. With the title, she especially wanted to call out that being blind can be an advantage in some situations.

This format of 'blind' interviews might not fit everyone. It might feel too bizarre or uncomfortable to do this. In that case, make sure to explore other opportunities to not be blinded by your preconceptions and biases. We suggest this could be done in a variety of ways and offer two examples below for you to try out.

### No visuals in online interviews

When using an online platform for interviews do the interviews without the camera on. Remember to also request to all candidates and interviewers to remove their profile photos.

## Publicly Available Resources

To learn more about this challenge, we recommend that you check out Gina Badenoch's TEDx talk called 'The Value of Eradicating Mental Blindness.'

Inclusive Interviewing

# Job Interview in Two Parts

## The Challenge

The job interview situation is influenced by bias and implicit norms. We are often seduced by those who are culturally recognisable, who fit the organisational norms, and who replicate the implicit norms for how to behave in a job interview. These norms are not explicit nor communicated. They are culturally specific and, as such, are an advantage for just a few people and a disadvantage for many people due to diverse backgrounds, cultures, personality types, and experiences.

Research[118] shows that we tend to ask the 'norm-fit' candidates less critical questions, and at the same time use more guiding micro-behaviours and encouraging micro-gestures (like nodding, sounds, smiles). The opposite is the case for candidates, who do not comply with the implicit norms. These are often instinctively rated as 'no hire' candidates. Unconsciously, we guide them less with encouraging micro-gestures and we ask them more critical questions. This gives them a poorer opportunity to perform in the interview than those we instinctively rate as 'yes hire' candidates. It is a challenge to change this during the interview because this is happening in the unconscious automatic system of the brain. When **Tinna C. Nielsen,** Founder of Move the Elephant for Inclusiveness, worked in a multinational organisation she designed and introduced this Inclusion Nudge to the managers.

### The Inclusion Nudge

Split the job interview into two parts, and evaluate between the two parts.

**Purpose:** Make it part of the evaluation and decision-making processes to challenge assumptions and bias about candidates by designing for a second chance for the recruitment panel to talk to the candidates and seek out facts to counter the assumptions, stereotypes, and biases.

## How To

The managers experimented with various ways to implement this de-biasing design in different kinds of interview situations. Here's how they often did it.

### ❶ Prepare
Inform the candidates about the two-part interview process and the purpose beforehand. The purpose is to ensure high quality of the interview process.

### ❷ Interview part one: the regular interview
Conduct the first part of the interview and follow a semi-structured interview guide. Then, the recruiting panel leaves the room and the candidate stays. Encourage the candidate to think about information they still need, and about any more examples that they want to share which will illustrate more about them in the second part of the interview.

### ❸ Mid-way check-in
*(about 5 minutes)*
This is not a discussion, but more of a quick 'check in'. The recruiting panel check if they have asked the questions and addressed the topics in the interview guide to be able to compare the candidates afterwards, and also have the information they need to evaluate the candidates fairly up against the qualification criteria. Also, they check if they need more information or facts about something. They then share first impressions about weak and strong sides. The recruitment panel members can also flag implicit associations and challenge these by asking **Flip Questions** like these. (To learn more about this, see **ASK FLIP QUESTIONS TO CHANGE YOUR PERCEPTIONS IN THE MOMENT** (→ page 143).

*"If 'he' was a 'she', then would we have thought the same?"*
*"If he had not had a two-year break, then would we have ...?"*
*"If she didn't have such a soft voice, then would we have listened differently?"*
*"If she had the same education as me, then would I have ...?"*

If the recruitment panel is familiar with using a rating scale of 1-5, then they can also do this. But make sure each member of the panel does their rating individually before sharing with each other. This is to avoid group conformity.

They can also use **default setting challenge questions**, such as *"If she is the best candidate, then why would she not be perfect for this job?"*

### ❹ Part two of the interview

The recruiting panel enters the interview room (where the candidate is waiting) again. They ask questions about issues that they need elaborated or ask for more examples of how the candidate works, etc. They also invite the candidate to ask questions.

### ❺ Final evaluation

The recruiting team makes the final evaluation (using individual, anonymous rating, again, to avoid group conformity). The recruiting team discusses arguments for both rejection and selection in relation to the qualification criteria – and checks for potential bias. Be sure to apply this approach consistently for all candidate interviews for the same position.

See the example about a Daniel Kahneman tool to structure and de-bias the evaluation and decision process called **STRUCTURED SCORING OF 6 QUALIFICATIONS** (→ page 126).

## Impact

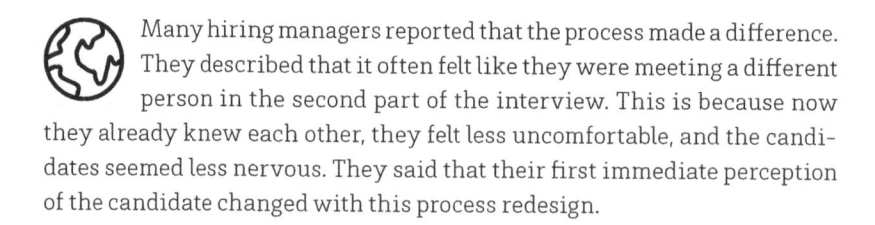

Many hiring managers reported that the process made a difference. They described that it often felt like they were meeting a different person in the second part of the interview. This is because now they already knew each other, they felt less uncomfortable, and the candidates seemed less nervous. They said that their first immediate perception of the candidate changed with this process redesign.

This design raises the level of reflection on biased conclusions. It reduced the tendency to primarily consider information that tended to confirm assumptions. The leaders also reported that they were less seduced by the candidates who were good at interviews, and it gave them a second chance to ask critical questions or ask for illustrative examples.

The recruitment panels that applied this process reported that it also changed how they perceived the candidates' merits. The process was more structured and professional. It also improved the ground for comparison of all candidates after the final evaluations. They also reported new insights about themselves and how quickly they relied on previous experiences and personal preferences.

## Authors' Comments & Behavioural Insights

### Why it works: behavioural insights

Taking a break helps to de-bias by protecting mental energy levels. Good decision-making using system 2 requires concentrated focus. Breaks allow for restoration of energy and dedicated time for reflection on what just occurred before moving forward. Breaks also help to interrupt mindlessness that a heavy **cognitive load** (due to the amount of information, the complexity of the task, etc.) can trigger. **Decision fatigue** can impact productivity, the quality of decisions, and achieving our intentions for equity.[119]

To achieve these benefits from breaks, it is important to **frame** the breaks as part of the process and the intention for better decision making of candidates. Otherwise, in the hyper-fast driven world that favours action over reflection **(action bias)**, the breaks can be diminished and skipped. Design breaks as an automatic part of the process. If there is resistance, then we suggest that you look at other framing actions that could be employed to support this process action. You can be inspired with ways to do this in the *Action Guide for Motivating Allies* and also in *The Inclusion Nudges Guidebook*.

The evaluation process phase of this Inclsuion Nudge could also include taking notice of the similarities and differences (diversity) that the candidates have relative to the current team and the organisation. See the *Framing Perceptions* Inclusion Nudge **DIFFERENCE AS CRITERION FOR SELECTION, NOT DE-SELECTION** (→ page 172).

**Inclusive Interviewing**

# Valuing Staff Contributions for Inclusive Culture

## The Challenge

**?** Many organisations state that diversity, equity, and inclusion are core to their 'DNA', values, and mission. The goal is often expressed that "everything we do is to create an inclusive culture". Yet, all too often, inclusive actions are not an expectation of all people in the organisation. Typically, the inclusive culture work is done by just a few people, usually by those in the minority groups and some in the majority group. This leads to inequality in the application of people's talent to create the culture that is desired and the organisation loses out on everyone's potential to be inclusive.

Additionally, there are penalties to people from minority groups who advocate for greater inclusion and equity. These include negative associations ('blame the messenger'), lower performance ratings, fewer career opportunities, higher stress, and lower employee engagement.[135]

By leaving diversity, equity, and inclusion change-making work to just a few and by positioning it as 'on top of the day job' carries significant risks to the organisation on loss of credibility (the intention-action gap), loss of talent potential, and not achieving the desired inclusive culture.

For an inclusive culture to be a reality, all people need to be engaged in achieving this on a daily basis. Additionally, the talent processes (hiring, promotion, performance evaluation, recognition, etc.) need to be designed in a way that makes inclusion the default for all to do and to be evaluated. Ways to do this are to have a prompter question on inclusive behaviours as a default in the interview questions and the performance appraisal process.

Here's how **Veronika Hucke**, Founder of D&I Strategy & Solutions, and **Lisa Kepinski,** Founder of Inclusion Institute, have shared with organisations on how to do this.

> **The Inclusion Nudge**
>
> Insert a prompter question within the performance appraisal process and in the job interview. Make this the default for all people.

**Purpose:** Ensure that everyone's contributions to an organisation's inclusion and diversity strategy are recognised and discussed as the default and norm, and thus being perceived as everybody's responsibility.

## How To

### Version 1: Talent selection process

Within the hiring process, write up the job description to include an expectation for inclusive behaviours in how employees do their work. Make this a default standard in all job descriptions by automatically having it as a part of the job description template (all are opted in on this text as they create a new job description).

Also, in the interview evaluation process include questions asking about how the applicant has been inclusive in past situations. Ask this of all applicants. Embed it in the application submission process (default standard question) and also in the interview questions asked of the candidates. Make 'inclusive behaviours' one of the talent selection criteria that is rated and considered in making the talent selection decision.

Inclusive culture is created by people doing inclusive behaviours (see the Inclusion Nudges INCLUSIVE Action Model pg 62). By integrating inclusive behaviours in the hiring process, you concretely show to all applicants, as well as to the interview committee members, that this is how work gets done in your organisation. It is what is expected of all and what is evaluated for all (not just a few people). Apply this process design to align the talent system to support hiring for the culture you want to have.

Here are some examples of questions that you could use.

*"How have you leveraged a diversity of perspectives and ideas in your work? What did you do and what was the outcome?"*

*"How have you ensured that all voices are heard in meetings that you participate in?"*

*"How have you empowered people that you work with? What did you do and what did you see happen as a result?"*

*"Have you ever seen or been told about discrimination or harassment in the organisation, and what did you do? What was the result? What would you do differently?"*

### Version 2: Talent performance review process

Within the performance appraisal process, include standard questions for all employees when they write up their accomplishments and development plans that cover their efforts beyond what is typically described as "their day job". Design the questions to cover both the formal company-related activities, **plus** other informal, relevant activities

The intent is to ensure that the performance appraisal process includes a wider view of what are "valued" employee contributions to the organisation and meaningful options for learning and skills development. The question, as part of the process, signals to employees and managers that the organisation recognises and rewards employees and leaders involvement in company initiatives, such as inclusion and diversity, and that this engagement is an advantage for the company. This shifts the perception of inclusion and diversity being a 'nice to have' to instead being core to the business and a viable investment of employees' time, which is recognised and rewarded by the organisation's managers.

Here are some examples of questions that you could use.

*"In addition to your formal objectives, identify contributions you have done to the make our workplace place more inclusive."*

*"How have you helped support making this a great place to work for all employees?"*

*"How do you make sure the diverse knowledge of your team members is being included to make stronger decisions and achieve our priorities?"*

While this *Process Design* Inclusion Nudge example is related to inclusion and diversity, the questions can be written in a broader way that encompasses a wide range of employee contributions to the organisation in other areas such as Corporate Social Responsibility, community volunteerism, employee and company events, customer-facing product launches, graduate student recruiting fairs, representing the company by speaking at events, and other special projects – all of which are aligned with the organisation's strategy but are outside of the formal role description or what is typically perceived as one's "day job".

## Impact

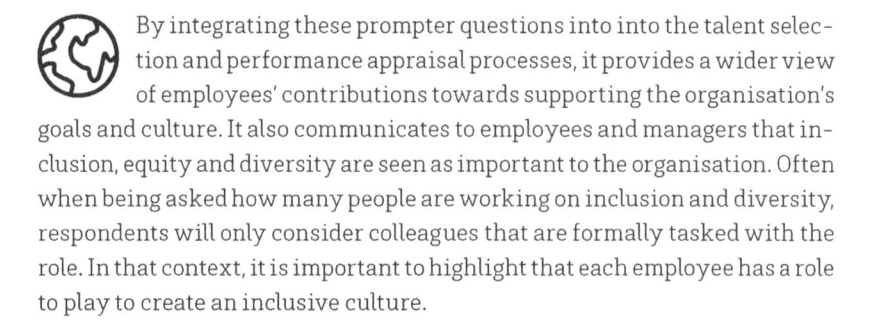

By integrating these prompter questions into into the talent selection and performance appraisal processes, it provides a wider view of employees' contributions towards supporting the organisation's goals and culture. It also communicates to employees and managers that inclusion, equity and diversity are seen as important to the organisation. Often when being asked how many people are working on inclusion and diversity, respondents will only consider colleagues that are formally tasked with the role. In that context, it is important to highlight that each employee has a role to play to create an inclusive culture.

By applying this Inclusion Nudge (combined with other Inclusion Nudges) you can make inclusion the norm – everywhere, for everyone, **and by everyone!**

> **WHAT & HOW**
> *I'll make sure to do inclusive interviewing*

SECTION 6

# How You Take This Forward

*How you can have impact on a new level*

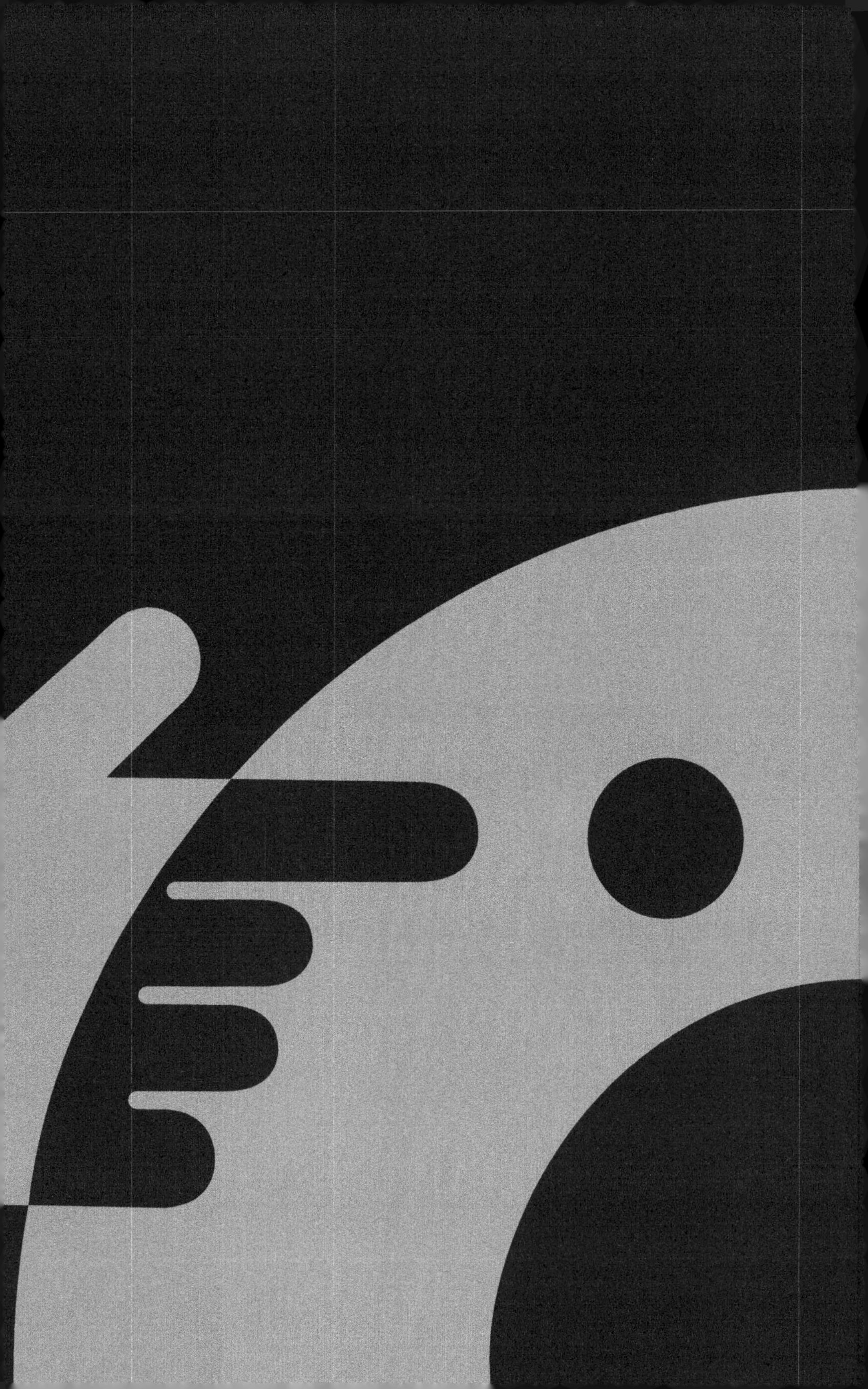

## How you get buy-in and support from others in making changes

You might experience, like we have many times, when you suggest changes in the way you normally select people for your teams, projects, and positions, or when you suggest changing the talent selection process design, that other people involved do not see a need for those changes. Perhaps you even meet resistance, or people working against the changes (or you). Instead of telling them that the current way of working and the process design are biased and not inclusive, and that this is at the risk of not selecting the best qualified based on merit, or even deselecting new talents needed, it is much more effective to *show* them the issues and make them *feel the need* to engage in the changes.

> Show, don't tell.
> As humans, we engage in change when we see and feel the need.
> Not by understanding the need.

This can be done in ways that motivate their unconscious mind to support the change for more inclusive talent selection. Examples of such motivational actions, that we call *Feel the Need* Inclusion Nudges, are in the *Action Guide for Motivating Allies* with 30 actions to get people engaged in promoting inclusive evaluation and selection, inclusive opportunities, inclusive collaboration, and inclusive society. There are also many more in the full version of *The Inclusion Nudges Guidebook* (2020). We encourage you to also get one of these publications to support your change efforts for more inclusive talent selection.

## Watch these TEDx talks for more inspiration

To experience the power of Inclusion Nudges, we recommend that you watch our TEDx talks where we illustrate how these work.

### TEDx Talk: Outsmarting Our Brains to Mitigate Bias in Talent Decisions
https://www.youtube.com/watch?v=4DpZm0GNqfQ

Hear how Lisa Kepinski addressed resistance from executives to increasing women in senior leadership. An interactive Inclusion Nudge helped them see the hidden patterns of unintentional exclusion and unequal opportunities. They moved from resistance to ownership, co-creation, and action-taking, resulting in several promotions of women in the next 6 months.

### TEDx Talk: Nudge Behaviour for a More Inclusive World
https://www.youtube.com/watch?v=VggAqa0x0wM

Take part in the interactive experiment that Tinna C. Nielsen is doing in the beginning of this talk. This is an example of a motivational Inclusion Nudge making people feel the need to change how they make judgements and decisions. The result is people taking active part in combating inequality by changing behaviours, cultures, and systems in their sphere of influence.

> **What are the challenges I experience (or suspect) we have in our talent selection processes?**

## How you make it happen

You can easily make inclusion the norm by applying the inclusive actions described in this Action Guide and using a process cycle of everyday experimentation to guide you. This is not only about talent selection processes, but about everything you do everyday. This is about the power we all have to make small changes with impact in our sphere of influence.

All steps in this process are needed; don't overlook any of them. This will ensure your commitment to action, your credibility that you do what you say you want to do, and your ability to be a more effective inclusive leader with impact.

Call upon your courage and go forward. You can make it happen!

*What and how I'll do this*

## INCLUSIVE TALENT SELECTION
## How you do everyday experimentations
## – step by step

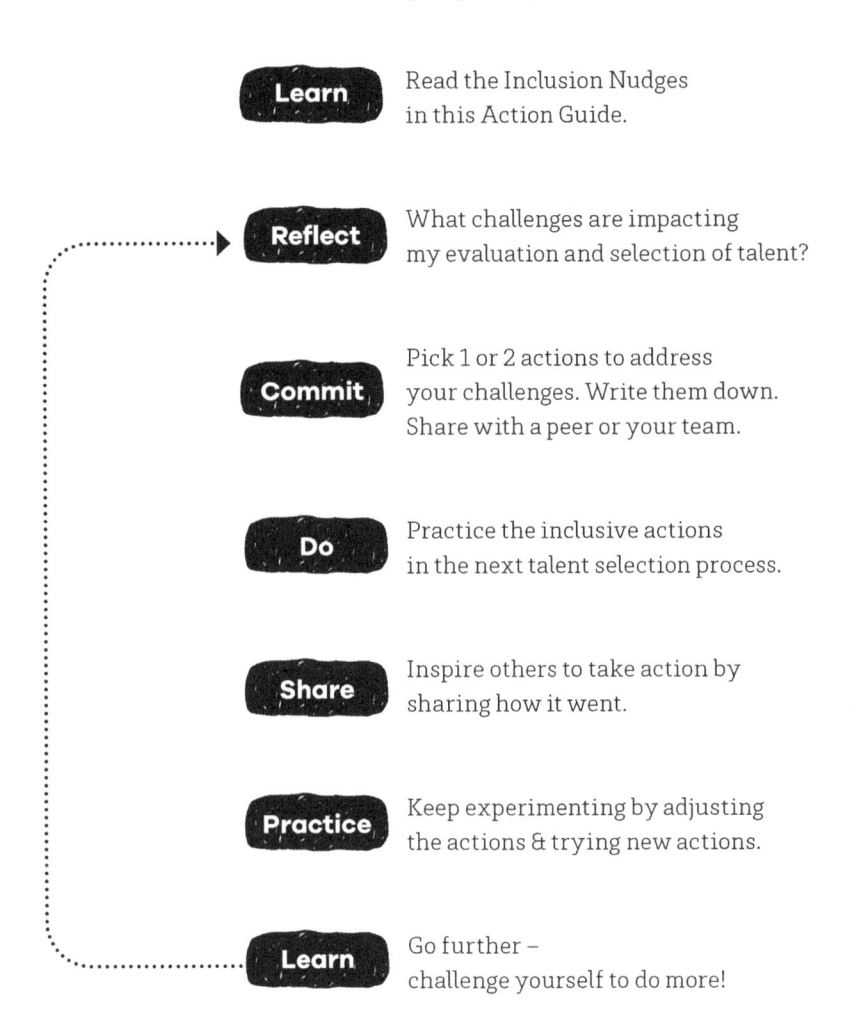

**Learn** — Read the Inclusion Nudges in this Action Guide.

**Reflect** — What challenges are impacting my evaluation and selection of talent?

**Commit** — Pick 1 or 2 actions to address your challenges. Write them down. Share with a peer or your team.

**Do** — Practice the inclusive actions in the next talent selection process.

**Share** — Inspire others to take action by sharing how it went.

**Practice** — Keep experimenting by adjusting the actions & trying new actions.

**Learn** — Go further – challenge yourself to do more!

There are many ways to take your learning forward. See the resources on the Inclusion Nudges resource platform www.inclusion-nudges.org

**KEEP LEARNING**

Get more Inclusion Nudge designs in the other books in this
**ACTION GUIDE SERIES**

### INCLUSION NUDGES FOR MOTIVATING ALLIES
Action Guide with 30 examples

**WHAT** Practical ways to show people issues of inequality, discrimination and unconscious bias that they are blind to, and to feel the need to engage in the change. As a result, they will automatically be allies.

**WHO** For you who are a leader, diversity, equity, and inclusion professional, human resource professional, social activist, human rights advocate, or member in an employee or citizen network or group. You want to motivate more people to get engaged in making changes in organisations and communities.

### INCLUSION NUDGES FOR LEADERS
Action Guide with 30 examples

**WHAT** Practical ways to enhance your leadership by leveraging diverse human potential and de-biasing processes, cultures, and behaviours to be inclusive as the norm.

**WHO** You who are leaders, formal and informal, managers, project leads, entrepreneurs, and decision makers in organisations of all sectors and in local and global communities of all kinds (online and in person).

Order your paperbacks or e-books now:
www.inclusion-nudges.org

## THE INCLUSION NUDGES GUIDEBOOK

### FOR CHANGE MAKERS – 100 Inclusion Nudges

**WHAT** For you who are a change maker, leader, developer, social activist or innovator leading change. You work on organisational or societal development, diversity, equity, inclusion, social impact, human resources, human rights, the UN Global Goal, and/or other areas of change for greater inclusivity. You want practical designs and inspiration to make impact. *The Inclusion Nudges Guidebook* is your comprehensive go-to resource to make inclusion happen with over 100 actions that you can do.

**WHO** For you who want to make changes for social impact, inclusion, diversity, gender parity, and equality, who work in human resources, are a diversity, equity, and inclusion professional, and in any other way leading change.

Order your paperback now:
www.inclusion-nudges.org

## Moving forward as a global community

From around the world, tens of thousands of leaders, project managers, change makers, human resource and diversity & inclusion professionals like you, are exploring how they can apply the Inclusion Nudges change approach in their processes of selecting talent and building diverse teams. This strengthens people, organisations, and communities by reducing the influence of bias and increases inclusivity. Their feedback has been overwhelmingly positive. Appreciation has been expressed for the impact and the evidence-based grounding in behavioural science as well as the real-life expertise of making inclusion, diversity, equity, and belonging a reality and the norm.

This Action Guide is a result of people sharing their experiences with applying Inclusion Nudge actions, including their own design variations, and the results. The *Action Guide for Talent Selection* is part of the Inclusion Nudges global initiative, with the purpose to leverage diverse human talents and potential, and creating more inclusive behaviour, culture, processes, and systems. We do this by applying behavioural insights and making inclusion the norm everywhere, for everyone.

Together, we can create a profound transformation in organisational and societal development to achieve more inclusive and sustainable development. You make it actionable.

All action matters, both in our own 'local' context and collectively in a 'global' context. We need to inspire and empower each other to make it happen. That's why reciprocal sharing of practical actions proven to work is important. It is why we founded this movement. We would be grateful to hear from you how you put the Inclusion Nudges in the Action Guide into action. Share how it works out.

Send us an email: contact@inclusion-nudges.org

Thank you, *Lisa & Tinna*

**Lisa Kepinski & Tinna C. Nielsen**

Founders of the Inclusion Nudges Global Initiative, Authors of *The Inclusion Nudges Guidebook* (2020) and *Inclusion Nudges Action Guide Series*

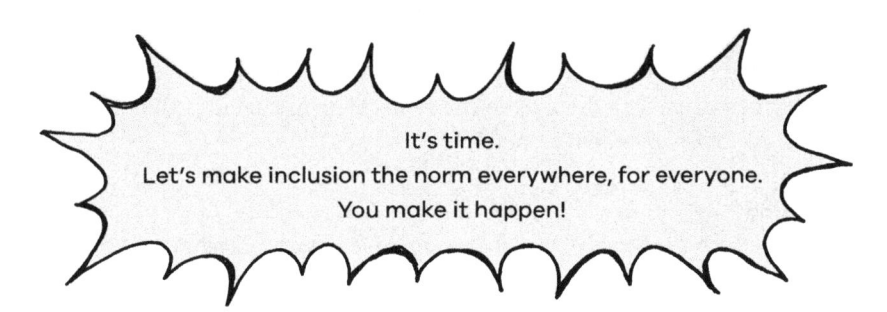

It's time.
Let's make inclusion the norm everywhere, for everyone.
You make it happen!

# Getting Clear on the Principles

## The Inclusion Nudges initiative principles

The global Inclusion Nudges change initiative is building on a very simple idea. When we (people who want to make changes) design interventions that nudge the unconscious mind to be inclusive by default, then Tinna and Lisa write exactly what and how it was done to make it work. Then, we share it with others who can then do it in their context. From this, we developed the global initiative for others to do the same. Here are some of the Inclusion Nudges global movement principles.

### Sharing
This initiative is based on collaboration, co-creation, and sharing to enable other change makers. Sharing what has worked for you is needed to keep this movement progressing. What you share inspires others and sparks global change to make inclusion the default and the norm. Without sharing, there is no initiative. Your insights and experiences are needed. Your colleagues in the global community are counting on you to do this.

### Reciprocity
You can make social change happen. Taking (benefiting) and sharing (giving to others) are important to enable as many people as possible to make inclusion the norm. You can do this by joining forces, exchanging knowledge, offering examples, and doing both 'give & get' and gift giving for the greater good. These are all vital ways to keep this movement going. And you are at the centre of this.

### Open source
The Inclusion Nudges initiative is for everybody. It is for those who want to use the examples being shared, those who design without applying, and those doing both. And it is for those who are curious and want to learn more. We all need ideas for what can work, and to be able to freely access this. This is why we didn't copyright the concept or approach. Knowledge shouldn't be hoarded to one's self or for sale to a select few, but shared with all in the world. That is how social change can happen.

Though we have coined the term 'Inclusion Nudge' and developed the framework of the three types of Inclusion Nudges, we have not copyrighted or trademarked these concepts because we believe in sharing, open source, and professional trust.

> In support of this approach, we have applied the Creative Commons Attribution-Non-Commercial-Share Alike 4.0 International license[136] to the Inclusion Nudges concept.
>
> Note that our writing in *The Inclusion Nudges Guidebook,* the Inclusion Nudges Action Guide Series books, and the Inclusion Nudges blog articles are under copyright permission.
>
> Citation: *"From Inclusion Nudges Action Guide Series © 2020 Tinna C. Nielsen and Lisa Kepinski. All rights reserved."*

Take a quick look at the next two pages for more information on how to apply these principles in practice.

## What's okay & what's NOT okay

Based on our experiences over the past couple of years as our Inclusion Nudges change methodology and the examples in the guidebook have spread globally, and the term Inclusion Nudges has grown in popularity, **we realise there is a growing need to clarify what sharing, reciprocity, and open source means. Some people seem to have misunderstood. So, here is what's okay and not okay.**[137]

**Thank you for honouring
the Inclusion Nudges initiative principles.**

| It's **okay** to use the Inclusion Nudge examples of your peers | It's **not okay** to use the examples and pretend it's your own design |

**Tell who designed it and where you got it from!**

| It's **okay** to experiment with the design of the Inclusion Nudge examples | It's **not okay** to keep the learning and outcome to yourself |

**Share with us how it worked for you!**

| It's **okay** to write about Inclusion Nudges in your own books and articles | It's **not okay** if you don't mention that you didn't come up with the concept |

**Tell people about the original source!**

| It's **okay** to use the examples to make change in your sphere of influence | It's **not okay** to use it for your own or your organisation's commercial use |

**Direct people to *The Inclusion Nudges Guidebook* to get the examples!**

| It's **okay** to tell your clients about Inclusion Nudges and give examples | It's **not okay** that you set up your consultancy based on the Inclusion Nudges concept |

**Use it in your work, but don't sell it like you created the concept!**

| It's **okay** to inform others about Inclusion Nudges | It's **not okay** that you keep it to yourself when you benefit from this |

**Tell others about the free resources on the website, so they benefit too!**

| It's **okay** to share in your network about Inclusion Nudges | It's **not okay** to share so you can sell it tied to a membership fee to your organisation |

**Tell all about the resources, but don't sell it or limit it to just a few!**

| It's **okay** that you tell about Inclusion Nudges in your presentations | It's **not okay** that you copy presentations designed & given by Lisa and Tinna |

**Make your own by being inspired – and reference the source!**

| It's **okay** that you see a need for the guidebook in other languages | It's **not okay** that you translate it without the authors' permission |

**Reach out to us to discuss opportunities for this!**

| It's **okay** to share about Inclusion Nudges on your organisation's platform | It's **not okay** to copy and paste direct text from the guidebook |

**Put the Inclusion Nudges website link on your platform!**

| It's **okay** to create a conference on Inclusion Nudges | It's **not okay** to do this without informing or involving Lisa and Tinna |

**Engage us to represent accurately the Inclusion Nudges methodology!**

| It's **okay** to be inspired and share the guidebook in your organisation | It's **not okay** to copy the guidebook and pass that around |

**Buy multiple copies of the guidebook and give as gifts to your colleagues!**

REFERENCE SECTION

# About the Authors

# Endnotes

"Never doubt that a small group
of thoughtful, committed citizens
can change the world;
indeed, it's the only thing that ever has."

Margaret Mead,
Anthropologist, 1901–1978

## About the authors

### Founders of the INCLUSION NUDGES global initiative

**Tinna C. Nielsen**

**Lisa Kepinski**

Founder
Move the Elephant
for Inclusiveness

Founder
Inclusion Institute

Lisa Kepinski and Tinna C. Nielsen co-authored *The Inclusion Nudges Guidebook* and co-founded the Inclusion Nudges global initiative in 2013. For this innovative work, Lisa and Tinna were named to The Economist's & The Telegraph's Global Diversity List "Top 10 List" in 2015, 2016, & 2017. Also, the Inclusion Nudges Initiative was shortlisted for a European Diversity Award in 2019. We also write for the World Economic Forum's blog Agenda.

{ To learn more or have a discussion, please contact.us at contact@inclusion-nudges.org }

## Tinna C. Nielsen

**Move the Elephant for Inclusiveness**
tinna@movetheelephant.org

Tinna is an anthropologist, social entrepreneur, and behavioural designer pioneering innovative approaches for practitioners, leaders and change makers to accelerate inclusiveness, diversity, gender parity, and equality as a means to achieve better innovation, collaboration, and sustainable development in our organisations, communities, cities, and societies.

For the past 19 years Tinna has specialised in applying insights from behavioural and social sciences to design impactful change in behaviours, cultures, and systems. Tinna has worked for the Danish Institute for Human Rights, and as Global Head of Inclusion, Diversity & Collaboration in Arla Foods (2010-2015), and in 2013, Tinna founded the change-organisation Move the Elephant for Inclusiveness, partnering with private and public organisations, NGOs, and governments worldwide, as well as collaborating with people at all levels of society and in all sectors. Tinna is also a strategic partner for inclusiveness and gender parity at the United Nations, as well as educating UN leaders and gender focal points. Tinna has extensive experience in inclusive leadership development at all levels and in all functions, and she is internationally recognised for her interactive style of influencing, teaching, facilitating, co-designing, and giving talks (TEDx talk in 2017). In addition to writing *The Inclusion Nudges Guidebook,* Tinna has co-authored social innovation books about how to redesign social welfare systems based on behavioural insights, and how to do citizen and community co-creation.

The World Economic Forum (WEF) honoured Tinna as a Young Global Leader (YGL) in 2015. She is taking part in the YGL community to create solutions to improve the state of the world. She served as co-chair of the WEF Global Future Council on Behavioural Sciences 2016-18, and is part of the WEF Expert Network, and a regular writer for the WEF blog Agenda. Tinna is Fellow at the RSA, Royal Society of Arts, serves on several advisory boards, as well as volunteering her support to social innovation initiatives where she lives and worldwide.

Tinna is now living in Denmark with her three daughters and husband.

# Lisa Kepinski

**Inclusion Institute**
lisa.kepinski@inclusion-institute.com

Lisa partners with organisations on how to successfully achieve their goals for creating a more inclusive culture for sustainable growth. Her deep expertise in organisational development and behavioural science integrated with inclusive culture make her a unique resource. With nearly 20 years' experience as a global inclusion & diversity executive for AXA, Microsoft, & HP, Lisa knows well the realities of creating change inside large, global organisations. With deep experience as an internal inclusion change leader, Lisa founded in 2013 the Inclusion Institute and focuses on designing organisational and behavioural change strategy and actions to increase inclusion, equity, and diversity. She also coaches change makers and leaders to enable them to carry this work forward in their organisations. Lisa's clients are from a wide range of sectors including multinationals, businesses, NGOs, governments, universities, and directly with individual change makers.

As an inclusion and behavioural change thought leader, Lisa frequently speaks at conferences, offers webcasts, and advises organisations. In June 2017, Lisa gave a TEDx talk on the need to design for inclusive behavioural change. She conducts research and writes to help further the practice of inclusion, equity, and diversity. Doing this always with a practical application focus. In addition to *The Inclusion Nudges Guidebook*, she has co-conducted global studies on improving the effectiveness of women networks, inclusion & diversity actions with impact (published by Newsweek), and most recently on inclusive remote work. Lisa works with groups to encourage their focus on inclusion, such as by serving on several advisory boards, chairing conferences, founding the Europe-based Global D&I Forum, and an expert panellist for Global Diversity & Inclusion Benchmarks.

Lisa has lived in 5 countries and travelled extensively in her global roles. She was born and educated in the US (with degrees in social psychology and socio-linguistics), has worked in Europe for over 20 years, has 2 adult daughters, and lives in Germany with her husband.

# Endnotes

1   **ARTICLE ON INCLUSION NUDGES.** Ellen McGirt, Fortune's RaceAhead: Culture and Diversity in Corporate America, 9 May 2019

2   To learn more about The Great Reset, see the World Economic Forum's strategic initiative resource: https://www.weforum.org/great-reset/?utm_source=sfmc&utm_medium=email&utm_campaign=2724334_Webinar_invite_july-expert_network&utm_term=&emailType=Webinar%20Invitation%e2%80%8b&sk=MDAxYjAwMDAwMGlU-enFYQUFT

3   **WHY DIVERSITY AND INCLUSION MATTER.** Research compilation by Catalyst, 1 August 2018; **WHY DIVERSE TEAMS ARE SMARTER.** David Rock & Heidi Grant, Harvard Business Review, 4 November, 2016; **NEURO-DIVERSITY AS A COMPETITIVE ADVANTAGE.** Robert D. Austin & Gary P. Pisano, Harvard Business Review, May-June 2017; **DIVERSITY MATTERS.** Vivian Hunt, Dennis Layton, & Sara Prince, McKinsey & Company, 2 February 2015; **HOW DIVERSITY MAKES US SMARTER.** Katherine W. Phillips, Scientific American, 1 October 2014; **THE DIFFERENCE: HOW THE POWER OF DIVERSITY CREATES BETTER GROUPS, FIRMS, SCHOOLS, AND SOCIETIES.** Scott E. Page, 2007

4   **THE POLITICS OF HAPPINESS. WHAT GOVERNMENT CAN LEARN FROM THE NEW RESEARCH ON WELL-BEING.** Derek Bok, 2011; **DEVELOPMENT AS FREEDOM.** Amartya Sen, 2001; **THE VILLAGE EFFECT: HOW FACE-TO-FACE CONTACT CAN MAKE US HEALTHIER AND HAPPIER.** Susan Pinker, 2015; **IMMUNOLOGY: THE PURSUIT OF HAPPINESS.** Nature, 27 November 2013; **WHAT'S GOOD FOR COMPANIES IS GOOD FOR NGOS TOO.** Tripathi, S. live-mint, 15 June 2015

5   **WHY INCLUSIVE LEADERS ARE GOOD FOR ORGANIZATIONS, AND HOW TO BECOME ONE.** Juliet Bourke & Andrea Espedido, Harvard Business Review, 29 March 2019

6   **BLINK: THE POWER OF THINKING WITHOUT THINKING.** Malcom Gladwell, 2007

7   **HEIGHT AND LEADERSHIP.** Erik Lindqvist, The Review of Economics and Statistics, vol 94, no 4, pgs 1191-1196, November 2012; **TALL CLAIMS? SENSE AND NONSENSE ABOUT THE IMPORTANCE OF HEIGHT OF US PRESIDENTS.** Gert Stulp, Abraham P. Buunk, Simon Verhulst, & Thomas V. Pollet, The Leadership Quarterly, vol 24, no 1, pgs 159-171, February 2013; **IN POLITICS, HEIGHT MATTERS.** The Economist, 19 February 2020

8   **CAMBRIDGE DICTIONARY.** 2020

9   **MACMILLAN DICTIONARY. 2020; MERRIAM-WEBSTER DICTIONARY. 2020; VOCABULARY.COM.** 2020

10   **HEIGHT AND LEADERSHIP.** Erik Lindqvist, The Review of Economics and Statistics, vol 94, no 4, pgs 1191-1196, November 2012

11   **HEIGHT AT AGE 18 YEARS IS A STRONG PREDICTOR OF ATTAINED EDUCATION LATER IN LIFE: COHORT STUDY OF OVER 950,000 SWEDISH MEN.** Patrik K.E. Magnusson, Finn Rasmussen, & Ulf B. Gyllensten, International Journal of Epidemiology, vol 35, no 3, pgs 658-663, 2006

12   **THE EFFECT OF PHYSICAL HEIGHT ON WORKPLACE SUCCESS AND INCOME.** Timothy A. Judge & Daniel M. Cable, Journal of Applied Psychology, vol 89, no 3, pgs 428-441, 2004; **THE EFFECT OF ADOLESCENT EXPERIENCE ON LABOR MARKET OUTCOMES: THE CASE OF HEIGHT.** Nicola Persico, Andrew Postlewaite, & Dan Silverman, Journal of Political Economy, vol 112, no 5, pgs 1019-53, 2004; **BLINK: THE POWER OF THINKING WITHOUT THINKING.** Malcom Gladwell, 2007, **SIZE MATTERS! BODY HEIGHT AND LABOR MARKET DISCRIMINATION: A CROSS-EUROPEAN ANALYSIS.** Francesco Cinnirella & Joachim Winter, CESifo Working Paper, no 2733, July 2009; **HEIGHT AND LEADERSHIP.** Erik Lindqvist, Review of Economics and Statistics, vol 94, no 835, January 2010; **THE FINANCIAL PERKS OF BEING TALL.** Joe Pinsker, The Atlantic, 18 May 2015; **HEIGHT, HUMAN CAPITAL, AND EARINGS: THE CONTRIBUTIONS OF COGNITIVE AND NONCOGNITIVE ABILITY.** Andreas Schick & Richard H. Steckel, Journal of Human Capital, vol 9, no 1, pgs 94-115, Spring 2015; **HEIGHT, BODY MASS INDEX, AND SOCIOECONOMIC STATUS: MENDELIAN RANDOMISATION STUDY IN UK BIOBANK.** Jessica Tyrrell, Samuel E. Jones, Robin Beaumont, Christina M. Astley, Rebecca Lovell, Hanieh Yaghootkar, et al, British Medical Journal, vol 352, 8 March 2016

13   **PERCEPTION OR REALITY? THE EFFECT OF STATURE ON LIFE OUTCOMES.** Jack Ludwig, Gallup, 12 September 2005

14   **HEIGHT DISCRIMINATION IN EMPLOYMENT.** Isaac B. Rosenberg, W&M Law School Student Publications, 2009

15   **DOES HEIGHT MAKE RIGHT? U.S. PRESIDENTS AND THEIR HEIGHT, WEIGHT, AND GREATNESS.** Timothy A. Judge, The Ohio State University Fisher College of Business Leadership Initiative Lead Read Today, 2 May 2018

16   **13 WORLD LEADERS RANKED BY HOW TALL THEY ARE.** Sinéad Baker, Business Insider, 22 August 2019

17   **PERCEPTION OR REALITY? THE EFFECT OF STATURE ON LIFE OUTCOMES.** Jack Ludwig, Gallup, 12 September 2005

18   **POWER LINKED TO PERCEPTION OF HEIGHT.** Rick Nauert, Association for Psychology Science, July 2015

19   **CAVEMEN POLITICS: EVOLUTIONARY LEADERSHIP PREFERENCES AND PHYSICAL STATURE.** Gregg R. Murray & J. David Schmitz, Social Science Quarterly, 18 October 2011; **HEIGHT, SOCIAL COMPARISON, AND PARANOIA: AN IMMERSIVE VIRTUAL REALITY EXPERIEMENTAL STUDY.** Daniel Freeman, Nicole Evans, Rachel Lister, Angus Antley, Graham Dunn, & Mel Slater, Psychiatry Research, vol 218, no 3, pgs 348-352, 30 August 2014

20   **THE RISE AND FALL OF POLITICIANS.** Philip A. Higham & William D. Carment, Canadian Journal of Behavioural Science, vol 24, pgs 404-409, 1992

21   **'I HAVE TO BE TALLER': THE UNREGULATED WORLD OF INDIA'S LIMB-LENGTHENING INDUSTRY.** Vidhi Doshi, The Guardian, 9 May 2016

22   **TRUMP'S HEIGHT BIAS.** New York Times, 22 October 2017

23   **THE AWFULNESS—AND AWESOMENESS—OF BEING SHORT.** BBC News, 29 September 2019; **SHORTCHANGED: HEIGHT DISCRIMINATION AND STRATEGIES FOR SOCIAL CHANGE.** Tanya S. Osensky, 2017

24   **THE RELATIONSHIP BETWEEN BODY WEIGHT AND PERCEIVED WEIGHT-RELATED EMPLOYMENT DISCRIMINATION: THE ROLE OF SEX AND RACE.** Mark V. Roehling, Patricia V. Roehling, & Shaun Pichler, Journal of Vocational Behavior, vol 71, no 2, pgs 300-318, 2007; **FOR BLACK MEN, BEING TALL INCREASES THREAT STEREOTYPING AND POLICE STOPS.** Neil Hester and Kurt Gray, PNAS, vol 115, no 11, pgs 2711-2715, January 2018; **THE EFFECTS OF SKIN TONE, HEIGHT, AND GENDER ON EARNINGS.** Srikant Devaraj, Narda R. Quigley, & Pankaj C. Patel, PLOS ONE, vol 13, no 1, 2018

25   **STUDY: BEING TALL IS A POSITIVE TRAIT FOR WHTE MEN; FOR BLACK MEN, NOT SO MUCH.** Trevor Lenzmeier, UNC Media Hub, 10 April 2018; **FOR BLACK MEN, BEING TALL INCREASES THREAT STEREOTYPING AND POLICE STOPS.** Neil Hester & Kurt Gray, Proceedings of the National Academy of Sciences of the United States of America, vol 115, no 11, pgs 2711-2715, 13 March 2018

26   **BLACK MALE STUDENT-ATHLETES AND RACIAL INEQUITIES IN NCAA DIVISION 1 COLLEGE SPORTS.** Shawn R. Harper, USC Race and Equity Center, 2018; **IT'S TIME TO ABONDON STEREOTYPES ABOUT BLACK STUDENT-ATHLETES.** David West, Jr., The Daily Texan, University of Texas at Austin, 12 April 2019; **MARCH MADNESS AND COLLEGE BASKETBALL'S RACIAL BIAS PROBLEM.** Steven Foy & Rashwan Ray, Brookings, 5 March 2020; **SKIN IN THE GAME: COLORISM AND THE SUBTLE OPERATION OF STEREOTYPES IN MEN'S COLLEGE BASKETBALL.** Steven Foy & Rashwan Ray, American Journal of Sociology, vol 125, no 3, November 2019; **"WHITE MEN CAN'T JUMP." BUT CAN THEY THROW? SOCIAL PERCEPTION IN EUROPEAN BASKETBALL.** Philip Furley & Matt Dicks, Stereotypes in European Basketball, 2014

27   **FOR BLACK MEN, BEING TALL INCREASES THREAT STEREOTYPING AND POLICE STOPS.** Neil Hester & Kurt Gray, Proceedings of the National Academy of Sciences of the United States of America, vol 115, no 11, pgs 2711-2715, 13 March 2018

28   **THE EFFECT OF SKIN TONE, HEIGHT, AND GENDER ON EARNINGS.** Srikant Devaraj, Narda R. Quigley, & Pankaj C. Patel, PLoS ONE, vol 13, no 1, 2018

29   **THE NUMBER OF FEMALE CHIEF EXECUTIVES IS FALLING.** Claire Cain Miller, New York Times, 23 May 2018

30   **LEADING WOMEN.** Nancy D. O'Reilly, 2014; **YOU HAVE NO CHOICE BUT TO LOOK UP TO THESE 17 TECH EXECS.** Alyson Shontell, Business Insider, 1 December 2012

31   **THE EFFECT OF SKIN TONE, HEIGHT, AND GENDER ON EARNINGS.** Srikant Devaraj, Narda R. Quigley, & Pankaj C. Patel, PLoS ONE, vol 13, no 1, 2018

32   **A SHORT NOTE ON ACCENT-BIAS, SOCIAL IDENTITY AND ETHNOCENTRISM.** Rahul Chakraborty, Advances in Language and Literary Studies, vol 8, no 4, 31 August 2017; **THE DETECTION OF FRENCH ACCENT BY AMERICAN LISTENERS.** James Emil Flege, Journal of Acoustical Society of America, vol 76, no 3, September 1984; **BRITISH ATTITUDES TOWARDS SIX VARIETIES OF ENGLISH IN THE USA AND BRITAIN.** Yuko Hiraga, World Englishes, vol 24, no 3, August 2005; **POLITICAL SKILL: EXPLAINING THE EFFECTS OF NONNATIVE ACCENT ON MANAGERIAL HIRING AND ENTREPRENEURIAL INVESTMENT.** Laura Huang, Marcia Frideger, & Jone L. Pearce, Journal of Applied Psychology, 12 August 2013

33   **A REPLICATION ATTEMPT OF STEREOTYPE SUSCEPTIBILITY.** Carolyn E. Gibson, Joy Losee, & Christine Vitiello, Social Psychology, vol 45, pgs 194-198, 2014; **PRIMING WHITE IDENTITY ELICITS STEREOTYPE BOOST FOR BIRACIAL BLACK-WHITE INDIVIDUALS.** Sarah E. Gaither, Jessica D. Remedios, Jennifer R. Schultz, & Samuel R. Sommers, Group Processes & Intergroup Relations, 2015; **THE EFFECT OF RACIAL PRIMES ON THE TEST PERFORMANCE OF AFRICAN-AMERICAN AND EUROPEAN-AMERICAN CHILDREN.** Jennifer R. Steele, Emily C. Bianchi, & Nalini Ambady, Revue internationale de psychologie sociale, vol 27, pgs 161-174, 2014; **TWENTY YEARS OF STEREOTYPE THREAT RESEARCH: A REVIEW OF PSYCHOLOGICAL MEDIATOR.** Charlotte R. Pennington, Derek Heim, Andrew R. Levy, & Derek T. Larkin, PLoS ONE, vol 11, no 1, 2016

34   **THIS PROBLEM HAS A NAME: DISCRIMINATION.** Marianne Bertrand, Chicago Booth Review, 21 May 2016

35   **WHITENED RÉSUMÉS: RACE AND SELF-PRESENTATION IN THE LABOR MARKET.** Sonia Kanga, Katy DeCelles, András Tilcsik, & Sora Jun, Administrative Science Quarterly, 22 January 2016; **ARE EMILY AND GREG MORE EMPLOYABLE THAN LAKISHA AND JAMAL? A FIELD EXPERIMENT ON LABOR MARKET DISCRIMINATION.** Marianne Bertrand & Sendhil Mullainathan, NBER Working Paper No.9873, July 2003

36   **NORTH AFRICAN IDENTITY AND RACIAL DISCRIMINATION IN FRANCE: A SOCIAL ECONOMIC ANALYSIS OF CAPABILITY DEPRIVATION.** Quentin Duroy, Review of Social Economy, vol 69, no 3, pgs 307-332, September 2011

37   **ARE EMPLOYERS IN BRITAIN DISCRIMINATING AGAINST ETHNIC MINORITIES?** GEMM Project & Centre for Social Investigation, 18 January 2019

38   **THE NAME-PRONUNCIATION EFFECT: WHY PEOPLE LIKE MR. SMITH MORE THAN MR. COLQUHOUN.** Simon M. Laham, Peter Koval, Adam L. Atler, Journal of Experimental Social Psychology, vol. 48, no 3, pgs 752-756, May 2012; **DRUNK TANK PINK.** Adam Alter, 2013; **WHAT YOUR NAME SAYS ABOUT HOW BELIEVABLE YOU ARE.** Matti Vuorre, Scientific American, 20 April 2014; **PEOPLE WITH EASIER TO PRONOUNCE NAMES PROMOTE TRUTHINESS OF CLAIMS.** Eryn J. Newman, Mevagh Sanson, Emily K. Miller, Adele Quigley-McBride, Jeffrey L. Foster, Daniel M. Bernstein, & Maryanne Garry, PLoS ONE, vol 9, no 2, 26 February 2014; **PREDICTING SHORT-TERM STOCK FLUCTUATIONS BY USING PROCESSING FLUENCY.** Adam L. Alter & Daniel M. Oppenheimer, PNAS, vol 103, no 24, pgs 9369-9372, 13 June 2006; **IF ITS DIFFICULT TO PRONOUNCE, IT MUST BE RISKY: FLUENCY, FAMILIARITY, AND RISK PERCEPTION.** Hyunjin Song & Norbert Schwarz, Psychological Science, 1 February 2009

39   **WISER: GETTING BEYOND GROUPTHINK TO MAKE GROUPS SMART.** Cass R. Sunstein & Reid Hastie, 2014; **MAKING DUMB GROUPS SMARTER.** Cass R. Sunstein & Reid Hastie, Harvard Business Review, December 2014; **HOW TO AVOID GROUPTHINK WHEN HIRING.** Atta Tarki, Harvard Business Review, 13 August 2019

40   **SEX DIFFERENCES: A STUDY IN THE EYE OF THE BEHOLDER.** John Condry & Sandra Condry, Child Development, vol 47, pgs 812–819, 1976

41   **GENDER-RELATED MATERIAL IN THE NEW CORE CURRICULUM.** Frank Flynn, Graduate School of Stanford Business News, 1 January 2007

42   **MENN SOM IKKE LIKER KARRIEREKVINNER.** Tarje Gaustad & Ketil Raknes, Markedshøyskolen & Tankesmien Agenda. February 2015

43   **THE FATHERHOOD BONUS AND THE MOTHERHOOD PENALTY: PARENTHOOD AND THE GENDER GAP IN PAY.** Michelle J. Budig, Third Way, 2 September 2014

44   **WHO GETS THE DADDY BONUS?: ORGANIZATIONAL HEGEMONIC MASCULINITY AND THE IMPACT OF FATHERHOOD ON EARNINGS.** M.J. Hodges, & M.J. Budig, Gender & Society, vol 24, no 6, pgs 717–745, 2010; **DISCRIMINATION IN HIRING BASED ON POTENTICAL AND REALIZED FERTILITY: EVIDENCE FROM A LARGE-SCALE FIELD EXPERIEMENT.** Sascha O. Becker, Ana Fernandes, & Doris Weichselbaumer, IZA Institute of Labor Economics, April 2019; **NORMATIVE DISCRIMINATION AND THE MOTHERHOOD PENALTY.** Stephen Benard & Shelley J. Correll, Gender & Society, vol 25, no 5, pgs 616-646, 2010; **MEN VIEWED MORE FAVORABLY THAN WOMEN WHEN SEEKING WORK-LIFE BALANCE.** Christin Munsch, American Sociological Association, 18 August 2014; **THE MOTHERHOOD PENALTY: WHY WE'RE LOSING OUT BEST TALENT TO CAREGIVING.** Shelley Zalis, Forbes, 22 February 2019; **MODERN FAMILY INDEX** 2018. Bright Horizons, 2019

45   **FOR WOMEN AND MINORITIES TO GET AHEAD, MANAGERS MUST ASSIGN WORK FAIRLY.** Joan C. Williams & Marina Mulhaup, Harvard Business Review, 5 March 2018; **WHEN GOOD DEEDS GO UNPUBLISHED.** Sarah Nightingale, UCR Today, 12 April 2017; **FACULTY SERVICE LOADS AND GENDER: ARE WOMEN TAKING CARE OF THE ACADEMIC FAMILY?** Cassandra M. Guarino & Victor M. H. Borden, Research in Higher Education, vol 58, pgs 672-694, 2017; **PRESCRIPTIVE STEREOTYPES AND WORKPLACE CONSEQUENCES FOR EAST ASIANS IN NORTH AMERICA.** Jennifer L. Berhdahl & Ji-A Min, Culture Diversity Ethnic Minor Psychology, vol 18, no 2, pgs 141-152, 2012; **REWARDING GOOD CITIZENS: THE RELATIONSHIP BETWEEN CITIZENSHIP BEHAVIOR, GENDER, AND ORGANIZATIONAL REWARDS.** Tammy D. Allen, Journal of Applied Social Psychology, vol 36, no 1, pgs 120-143, 2006; **GENDER DIFFERENCES IN ACCEPTING AND RECEIVING REQUESTS FOR TASKS WITH LOW PROMOTABILITY.** Linda Babcock, Maria P. Recalde, Lise Versterlund, & Laurie Weingart, American Economic Review, vol 107, no 3, pgs 714-47, March 2017

46   **WE ALL KNOW WORKPLACE DIVERSITY MAKES SENSE: SO WHY IS CHANGE SO SLOW?** Tinna Nielsen, World Economic Forum, 14 March 2016; **WOMEN IN THE WORKPLACE.** McKinsey, 2019; **WHY DIVERSITY PROGRAMS FAIL.** Frank Dobbin & Alexandra Kalev, Harvard Business Review, July-August 2016

47   **THE SURPRISING POWER OF SIMPLY ASKING COWORKERS HOW THEY'RE DOING.** Karyn Twaronite, Harvard Business Review, 28 February 2019

48   **NEW STUDY: 3 IN 5 U.S. EMPLOYEES HAVE WITNESSED OR EXPERIENCED DISCRIMINATION.** Glassdoor, 22 October 2019; **DIVERSITY & INCLUSION STUDY 2019.** Glassdoor, 29-31 July 2019

49   **MORAL SELF-LICENSING: WHEN BEING GOOD FREES US TO BE BAD.** Anna C. Merritt, Daniel A. Effron, and Benoıt Monin. Stanford University Social and Personality Psychology Compass 4/5: 344–357, 2010

50   **MORAL CREDENTIALS AND THE EXPRESSION OF PREJUDICE** Benoit Monin and Dale T. Miller. Journal of Personality and Social Psychology, Vol. 81, No. 1, 33-43, 2001

51   **SINNING SAINTS AND SAINTLY SINNERS THE PARADOX OF MORAL SELF-REGULATION.** Sachdeva, Sonya & Iliev, Rumen & Medin, Doug. Psychological science. 20. 523-8, 2009

52 **NUDGE.** Thaler & Sunstein, pg 6, 2008

53 **CUES OF BEING WATCHED ENHANCE COOPERATIONS IN A REAL-WORLD SETTING.** Melissa Bateson, Daniel Niettle, & Gilbert Roberts, Biology Letters, vol 2, pgs 412-14, 2016

54 **ACCOUNTABILITY: A SOCIAL CHECK ON THE FUNDAMENTAL ATTRIBUTION ERROR.** Philip E. Tetlock, Social Psychology Quarterly, vol 48, no 3, pgs. 227-236, 1985

55 **GENDER DIFFERENCES IN EMPLOYMENT,** OECD Family Database Social Policy Division – Directorate of Employment, Labour and Social Affairs, 30 June 2019

56 **FLEXIBLE WORKING: THE WAY OF THE FUTURE.**
Joy Burnfor, Forbes, 28 May 2019

57 **GLOBAL ANYWHERE WORKING.** Polycom, Inc, 2017

58 According to FlexJobs' sixth annual survey of more than 5,500 respondents in the US, citied in 2017 **ANNUAL SURVEY FINDS WORKERS ARE MORE PRODUCTIVE AT HOME,** Brie Weller Reynolds, 21 August 2017

59 **DAVOS EXPERTS SAYS ITS TIME TO SWITCH TO A F OUR-DAY WORK WEEK.** Ross Chainey, World Economic Forum Agenda, 25 January 2019

60 **FOUR-DAY WORKWEEK BOOSTED PRODUCTIVITY BY 40 %, MICROSOFT JAPAN EXPERIMENT SHOWS.** Kazuaki Nagata, The Japan Times, 5 November 2019

61 See research on default design and opt in opt out choices: **DEFAULTS, FRAMING, AND PRIVACY: WHY OPTING IN OPTING OUT.** Peterson Row. E.J. Johnson, S. Bellman, & G.L. Lohse, Marketing Letters, vol 13, pgs 5–15, 2002; **DO DEFAULTS SAVE LIVES?.** E.J. Johnson & D. Goldstein, Science, vol 302, pgs 1338–1339, 2003; **STATUS QUO BIAS IN DECISION MAKING.** W. Samuelson & R. Zeckhauser, Journal of Risk & Uncertainty, vol 1, pgs 7–59, 1988; **NUDGE: IMPROVING DECISIONS ABOUT HEALTH, WEALTH, AND HAPPINESS.** R.H. Thaler & C.R. Sunstein, 2008

62 **CASE STUDY: AN INSIDE LOOK AT TELSTRA'S FLEXIBLE WORKING PROGRAM.** Human Resources, 19 July 2017; **CASE STUDY: TELSTRA – ALL ROLES FLEX.** Catalyst, 12 April 2017; **TELSTRA EMPOWERS ITS EMPLOYEES TO DO THEIR BEST WORK FORM ANYWHERE WITH MICROSOFT OFFICE 365.** Gregory Koteras, general manager of digital workplace solutions at Telstra, shares what's worked for Telstra from a technology side to enable all roles flex

63 Justesen, 2011

64 Gratton et. al., 2007

65 See innoversity.org for more research results

66 **BAKER MCKENZIE FIRST GLOBAL LAW FIRM TO SET 40:40:20 GENDER TARGETS.** Baker McKenzie website, 24 June 2019

67 *Based on several sources including:* Susznne Justesen, **2011; INNOVATION: WHAT'S DIVERSITY GOT TO DO WITH IT?** Waverly Deutsch, Chicago Booth Review, 14 November 2019

68 **THE FRAMING OF DECISIONS AND THE PSYCHOLOGY OF CHOICE.** Amos Tversky & Daniel Kahneman, Science, vol 211, pgs 453-58, 1981

69  **JUDGEMENT UNDER UNCERTAINTY: HEURISTICS AND BIASES.** Amos Tversky & Daniel Kahneman, Science, vol 185, pgs 1124-31, 1974

70  **TWENTY YEARS OF STEREOTYPE THREAT RESEARCH: A REVIEW OF PSYCHOLOGICAL MEDIATORS.** Charlotte R. Pennington, Derek Heim, Andrew R. Levy, & Derek T. Larkin, Marina A. Pavlova, Editor, PLoS One, vol 11, no 1, 2016

71  *Based on several sources including:* **"MATH IS HARD!" THE EFFECT OF GENDER PRIMING ON WOMEN'S ATTITUDES.** Jennifer R. Steele, Journal of Experimental Social Psychology, vol 42, no 4, pgs 428-436, July 2006; **THE INFLUENCE OF GENDER STEREOTYPE THREAT ON MATHEMATICS TEST SCORES OF DUTCH HIGH SCHOOL STUDENTS: A REGISTERED REPORT.** Paulette C. Flore, Joris Mulder, & Jelte M. Wicherts, Comprehensive Results in Social Psychology, vol 3, no 2, pgs 140-174, 2018

72  *Based on several sources including:* **THIN ICE: "STEREOTYPE THREAT" AND BLACK COLLEGE STUDENTS.** C. M. Steele, The Atlantic Monthly, vol 284, no 2, pgs 44-47, 50-54, August 1999; **STEREOTYPE THREAT AND THE INTELLECTUAL TEST PERFORMANCE OF AFRICAN-AMERICANS.** C.M. Steele & J. Aronson, Journal of Personality and Social Psychology, vol 69, pgs 797-811, 1995; **THE UPS AND DOWNS OF ATTRIBUTIONAL AMBIGUITY: STEREOTYPE VULNERABILITY AND THE ACADEMIC SELF-KNOWLEDGE OF AFRICAN-AMERICAN STUDENTS.** J. Aronson & M. Inzlicht, Psychological Science, vol 15, pgs 829-836, 2004

73  **HOW SOCIAL-CLASS STEREOTYPES MAINTAIN INEQUALITY.** Federica Durante & Susan T. Fiske, Current Opinion in Psychology, vol 18, pg 43-48, December 2017

74  *Based on several sources including:* **STEREOTYPE THREAT INCREASES THE LIKELIHOOD THAT FEMALE DRIVERS IN A SIMULATOR RUN OVER JAYWALKERS.** N.C. Yeung & C. von Hippel, Accident Analysis and Prevention, vol 40, no 2, pgs 667-74, March 2008; **THE IMPACT OF STEREOTYPE THREAT ON THE SIMULATED DRIVING PERFORMANCE OF OLDER DRIVERS.** M Joanisse, S. Gagnon, & M. Voloaca, Accident Analysis and Prevention, vol 50, pgs 530-8, January 2013

75  **EVERYONE STARTS WITH AN A. APPLYING BEHAVIOURAL INSIGHT TO NARROW THE SOCIOECONOMIC ATTAINMENT GAP IN EDUCATION,** Nathalie Spencer, Jonathan Rowson, & Louise Bamfield, RSA Report, March 2014

76  **LONG-TERM EFFECTS OF SUBLIMINAL PRIMING ON ACADEMIC PERFORMANCE.** Brian S. Lowery, Naomi I. Eisenberger, Curtis D. Hardin, & Stacey Sinclair, Basic and Applied Social Psychology, vol 29, no 2, pgs 151-157, 2007

77  **LANGUAGE MATTERS: HOW WORD IMPACT MEN AND WOMEN IN THE WORKPLACE.** Report from LinkedIn, 2019

78  **'AGGRESSIVE' WOMEN NEED NOT APPLY: WHY THE LANGUAGE OF JOB POSTINGS MATTERS SO MUCH.** Natalie Sachmechi, Forbes, 1 August 2019

79  **GDIQ SPELLCHECK BIAS.** Vimeo: https://vimeo.com/361818349

80  **GEENA DAVIS ANNOUNCES 'SPELLCHECK FOR BIAS' TOOL TO REDRESS GENDER IMBALANCE IN MOVIES.** Andrew Pulver, The Guardian, 9 October 2019

81  **WHY PEOPLE WITH DISABILITIES ARE YOUR COMPANY'S UNTAPPED RESOURCE.** Thorkil Sonne, World Economic Forum Agenda, 10 January 2019

82  **NEURODIVERSITY AS A COMPETITIVE ADVANTAGE.** Robert D. Austin & Gary P. Pisano, Harvard Business Review, May-June 2017

83   **NEURODIVERSITY AS A COMPETITIVE ADVANTAGE.** Robert D. Austin & Gary P. Pisano, Harvard Business Review, May-June 2017

84   **IMPLICIT STEREOTYPING AGAINST PEOPLE WITH DISABILITY.** O. Rohmer & E. Louvet, Group Processes & Intergroup Relations, vol 21, no 1, pgs 127–140, 2018

85   **CAUSAL EFFECT OF INTERGROUP CONTACT ON EXCLUSIONARY ATTITUDES.** Ryan D. Enos, PNAS, vol 111, no 10, pgs 3699-3704, 11 March 2014

86   **APPLYING BEHAVIOURAL INSIGHTS TO CHARITABLE GIVING.** The UK Behavioural Insights Team & the Charites Aid Foundation

87   At the time of the campaign, Isis's last name was Wenger.

88   **YOU MAY HAVE SEEN MY FACE ON BART.** Isis Anchalee, Medium, 2 August 2015

89   **#ILOOKLIKEANENGINEER AIMS TO SPREAD AWARENESS ABOUT DIVERSITY IN TECH.** Megan Rose Dickey, Tech Crunch, 4 August 2015

90   **#ILOOKLIKEANENGINEER ADS START GOING UP IN THE BAY AREA THIS WEEK!** Michelle Glauser, Medium 14 September 2015

91   **THE STORIES OF THE #ILOOKLIKEANENGINEER COMMUNITY GATHERING.** Michelle Glauser, Medium, 28 August 2015

92   **THE BEST TWEETS FROM THE #ILOOKLIKEANENGINEER HASHTAG.** Fiona MacDonald, Science Alert, 6 August 2015

93   **#ILOOKLIKEANENGINEER: USING SOCIAL MEDIA-BASED HASHTAG ACTIVISM CAMPAIGNS AS A LENS TO BETTER UNDERSTAND ENGINEERING DIVERSITY ISSUES.** Aqdas Malik, Aditya Johri, Rajat Handa, Habib Karbasian, & Hermant Purohit, conference paper presented at The Collaborative Network of Engineering and Computing Diversity Conference held at Crystal City, Virginia, U.S.A., May 2018

94   **#ILOOKLIKEANENGINEER: ONE YEAR LATER.** Isis Anchalee, Medium, 3 August 2016

95   **NEW CHAPTERS: WHY I'M LEAVING SILICON VALLEY.** Isis Anchalee, Making Love With Life blog, 22 January 2019

96   **FEMALE LIBRARIANS AND MALE COMPUTER PROGRAMMERS? GENDER BIAS IN OCCUPATIONAL IMAGES ON DIGTIAL MEDIA PLATFORMS.** Vivek K. Singh, Mary Chayko, Raj Inamdar, & Diana Floegel, Journal Association of Information Science & Technology, pgs 1-14, 22 January 2020

97   **COUNTERING THE NEGATIVE IMAGE OF WOMEN IN COMPUTING.** Fay Cobb Payton & Eleni Berki, The Association for Computing Machinery, vol 62, no 5, pgs 56-63, May 2019

98   **SEEING IS BELIEVING: EXPOSURE TO COUNTER STEREOTYPIC WOMEN LEADERS AND ITS EFFECT ON THE MALLEABILITY OF AUTOMATIC GENDER STEREOTYPING.** Nilanjana Dasgupta & Shaki Asgari, Journal of Experimental Social Psychology, vol 40, pgs 642-658, 2014

99   **SUCCESSFUL FEMALE LEADERS EMPOWER WOMEN'S BEHAVIOR IN LEADERSHIP TASKS.** Ioana M. Latu, Marianne Schmid Mast, Joris Lammers, & Dario Bombari, Journal of Experimental Social Psychology, vol 49, pgs 444-448, 2013

100  **AMBIENT BELONGING: HOW STEREOTYPICAL CUES IMPACT GENDER PARTICIPATION IN COMPUTER SCIENCE.** Sapna Cheryan, Victoria C. Plaut, Paul G. Davies, & Claude M. Steele. Journal of Personality and Social Psychology, vol 97, pgs 1045-60, 2009

101  **COLLEGES HAVE INCREASED WOMEN COMPUTER SCIENCE MAJORS. WHAT CAN GOOGLE LEARN?** Laura Sydell, NPR, 10 August 2017

102  **FEMALE DOCTORS SAYING 'I LOOK LIKE A SURGEON'.** BBC, 15 August 2015

103  The statement and Daniel Kahneman's inspiration came from: **CLINICAL VERSUS STATISTICAL PREDICTION: A THEORETICAL ANALYSIS AND A REVIEW OF THE EVIDENCE.** Paul E. Meehl, 1954

104  **THINKING, FAST AND SLOW.** Daniel Kahneman, pgs 229-233, 2011

105  **SHE JUST DOESN'T LOOK LIKE A PHILOSOPHER ...? AFFECTIVE INFLUENCES ON THE HALO EFFECT IN IMPRESSION FORMATION.** Joseph P. Forgas, European Journal of Social Psychology, vol 41, pgs 812–817, 2011

106  **BLIND RECRUITMENT TRIAL TO BOOST GENDER EQUALITY MAKING THINGS WORSE, STUDY REVEALS.** Henry Belot, ABC, 30 Jun 2017; **UNINTENDED EFFECTS OF ANONYMOUS RESUMES.** Luc Behaghel, Bruno Crépon, & Thomas Le Barbanchon, IZA Discussion Papers, no 8517, Institute for the Study of Labor (IZA), Bonn, 2014

107  **HALO EFFECTS.** Joseph P. Forgas & Simon M. Laham, Encyclopedia of Social Psychology, January 2009

108  **BLINDED BY BEAUTY: ATTRACTIVENESS BIAS AND ACCURATE PERCEPTIONS OF ACADEMIC PERFORMANCE.** S.N. Talamas, K.L. Mavor, & D.L. Perrett, Plos one, vol 11, no 2, 2016

109  **NAME STEREOTYPES AND TEACHERS' EXPECTATIONS** H. Harari, & McDavid, J.W. Journal of Educational Psychology, vol 65, no 2, pgs 222-225, 1973

110  **TOP FLUTIST SETTLES GENDER PAY-GAP SUIT WITH BOSTON SYMPHONY ORCHESTRA.** Anastasia Tsioulcas, NPR, 21 February 2019

111  **THE HEIGHT LEADERSHIP ADVANTAGE IN MEN AND WOMEN: TESTING EVOLUTIONARY PSYCHOLOGY PREDICTIONS ABOUT THE PERCEPTIONS OF TALL LEADERS.** N.M. Blacker et al., Group Processes Intergroup Relations, vol 16, no 1, pgs 17-27, January 2013

112  **THE VALIDITY AND UTILITY OF SELECTION METHODS IN PERSONNEL PSYCHOLOGY: PRACTICAL AND THEORETICAL IMPLICATIONS OF 85 YEARS OF RESEARCH FINDINGS.** F. Schmitt & J. Hunter, Psychological Bulletin, vol 124, no 2, pgs 262-274, 1998

113  **THE EFFECT OF PURCHASE QUANTITY AND TIMING ON VARIETY SEEKING BEHAVIOUR.** I. Simonson, Journal of Marketing Research, vol 32, pgs 150-162, 1990

114  **HOW WE'RE FIGHTING UNCONSCIOUS BIAS.** Lindsay Grenawalt, Cockroach Labs Blog, 26 January 2017

115  **CREATING A FAIR HIRING PROCESS.** Dave Delaney, Cockroach Labs Blog, 9 October 2019

116 **UPDATING YOUR ENGINEERING INTERVIEW TO MAKE BETTER HIRING DECISIONS.** Lindsay Grenawalt, Cockroach Labs Blog, 17 May 2018

117 **AUTOMATICITY OF SOCIAL BEHAVIOR: DIRECT EFFECTS OF TRAIT CONSTRUCT AND STEREOTYPE ACTIVATION ON ACTION.** John A. Bargh, Mark Chen, and Lara Burrows, Journal of Personality and Social Psychology, vol 71, pgs 230-44, 1996

118 **JOBSAMTALER MED ETNISKE MINORITETER.** Iben Jensen, 2014

119 **EXTRANEOUS FACTORS IN JUDICIAL DECISIONS.** Shai Danziger, Jonathan Levav, & Liora Avnaim-Pesso, PNAS, vol 108, no 17, pgs 6889-6892, 26 April 2011; **BRIEF AND RARE MENTAL 'BREAKS' KEEP YOU FOCUSED: DEACTIVATION AND REACTIVATION OF TASK GOALS PREEMPT VIGILANCE DECREMENTS.** A. Ariga & A. Lleras, Cognition, 2011; **WHY YOUR BRAIN NEEDS MORE DOWNTIME.** Ferris Jabr, Scientific American, 15 October 2013

120 **THE HAWTHORNE STUDIES.** Historical sources at Harvard University: https://www.library.hbs.edu/hc/hawthorne/rl-selected.html#SDHR

121 **CUES OF BEING WATCHED ENHANCE COOPERATION IN A REAL-WORLD SETTING.** Melissa Bateson, Daniel Nettle, & Gilbert Roberts, Biology Letters, vol 2, pgs 412-4, 2006

122 **SEEING IS BELIEVING: THE ANTI-INFERENCE BIAS.** Eyal Zamir, Ilana Ritov, & Doron Teichman, Indiana Law Journal, 21 April 2012

123 **AWARENESS REDUCES RACIAL BIAS.** Devin G. Pope, Joseph Price, & Justin Wolfers, Management Science, vol 64, no 11, pgs 4988-4995, 2018. NOTE: We do believe that their evidence provides insights that it's not so much 'awareness of bias' but it's seeing the gap between their self-perception as professional referees and their biases behaviour, that helps systems 1 and 2 close the gap and reduce bias in the unconscious, automatic mind (calling the fouls in basketball).

124 **THE POWER OF PERSPECTIVE-TAKING.** Gillian Ku & Kathy Brewis, London Business School Review, 1 February 2017

125 **WISER.** Cass Sunstein and Reid Hastie, pgs 114-115, 2015

126 **THE HEART OF CHANGE.** John Kotter & Dan Cohen, 2002

127 **SWITCH.** Dan Heath & Chip Heath, pgs 12-15 & 105-107, 2010

128 **UNITED NATIONS VIRTUAL REALITY PROJECT.** https://www.digitaltrends.com/virtual-reality/un-using-virtual-reality/ and http://unvr.sdgactioncampaign.org//

129 **OVERLOOKED LEADERSHIP POTENTIAL: THE PREFERENCE FOR LEADERSHIP POTENTIAL IN JOB CANDIDATES WHO ARE MEN VS. WOMEN.** Abigail Player, Georgina Randsley de Moura, Ana Leite, Dominic. Abrams, & Fatima Tresh, Frontiers in Psychology, vol 10, pg 755, 16 April 2019

130 **DESCRIPTION AND PRESCRIPTION: HOW GENDER STEREOTYPES REVENT WOMEN'S ASCENT UP THE ORGANISATIONAL LADDER.** Madeline E. Heilman, Journal of Social Issues, vol 57, no 4, pgs 657-674, 2001

131 **JUDGEMENT UNDER UNCERTAINTY: HEURISTICS AND BIASES.** Amos Tversky & Daniel Kahneman, Science, 27 September 1974

132 **HOW SOCIAL INFLUENCE CAN UNDERMINE THE WISDOM OF CROWD EFFECT.** Jan Lorenz, Heiko Rauhut, Frank Schweitzer, & Dirk Helbing, Proceedings of the National Academy of Sciences of the United States of America (PNAS), 31 May 2011

133 **LIMITS FOR THE PRECISION AND VALUE OF INFORMATION FROM DEPENDENT SOURCES.** Robert T. Clemen & Robert L. Winkler, Operations Research, vol 33, no 2, pgs 427-442, March-April 1985

134 **WISER: GETTING BEYOND GROUPTHING TO MAKE GROUPS SMARTER.** Cass R. Sunstein & Reid Hastie, pg 2, 2014

135 **A FRESH LOOK AT WOMEN NETWORKS GLOBAL SURVEY REPORT.** Veronika Hucke & Lisa Kepinski, January 2016. Report available from the authors.

136 To review the Creative Commons license, go to: http://creativecommons.org/licenses/by-nc-sa/4.0/

137 While the content is based on the authors' own experience with Inclusion Nudges (the Guidebook, the community, and the website), there was inspiration on this section from Kelly Rae Roberts' website on *'what is and is not okay'* and also from the Global Diversity & Inclusion Benchmark (GDIB) website's permission agreement.